TAUGHT ME ABOUT
JESUS

WHAT MY DOG
TAUGHT ME ABOUT
JESUS

David Ross Sherman

Library of Congress Control Number:		2017908124
ISBN:	Hardcover	978-1-5434-2476-8
	Softcover	978-1-5434-2475-1
	eBook	978-1-5434-2474-4

All scripture references used are in the New King James Version of the bible unless otherwise noted.

Print information available on the last page.

Rev. date: 05/23/2017

To order additional copies of this book, contact:
Xlibris
1-888-795-4274
www.Xlibris.com
Orders@Xlibris.com
756312

CONTENTS

PREFACE

WHEN I LOOK at my dog, I wonder if she is wondering, *Do I know something you don't know, or is it that you know something I don't know?* And then I wonder if either of those is true.

I know that she is one the most joyful creatures I have ever known, so she knows how to be joyful and, like most of us, has some moments of sadness as well. As far as I know, she has never had any life traumas that would have affected her, unless you consider being born on the White Mountain Apache lands (where, I have heard it said, dog is a very tasty meal) and then being put in a doggy jail for nearly two years in and out, in and out—just for being born. Once a nice man took her home and brought her back in a few months. Her crime? She shed too much. They shaved her. I'm sure she understood. They had their reasons.

After her hair grew back was when I met her. Approaching retirement, I decided I needed to get a dog. I just wanted a friend to hang with me all day long, who would listen to me and would never want to add anything to the conversation but listen intently to all I had to say simply because it was me who was saying it. So it would have to be a stupid dog or at least one who was a good actor. Jenny is neither stupid, nor is she an actress. She is always real. And she is very intelligent. Yet she hangs with me all day long and listens to me and rarely adds anything to the conversation. She often listens intently as I speak and yet sometimes ignores me, unless, of course, I have that tone that commands attention.

I am a pastor, so Jenny is always the first to hear any message I prepare; and I discuss with her many things regarding God and His creation. Jenny knows that she is created to serve, and she does it without complaint because she knows and accepts her role. Jenny has shown me that if we know our roles in this life and perform those roles to the best of our ability, we are rewarded.

That's why I wrote this book. If we take the time to notice all creation in all its forms, we will discover that it screams out to us to discover God. He is everywhere and in everything. He is found in every plant, every mineral, and every rock. And yes, He is found in animals.

Animals are no less a gift from God than anything else, but they are probably less appreciated by some. Some folks have a lessened appreciation of some things, and that's just fine. But I heard once that if we seek God, we will find Him. And what I have learned in my more than thirty years of seeking is that we can find Him everywhere simply because that is where He is—in everything. I believe God has created all things. That is inclusive of animals (just making sure we're on the same page). Animals truly give us some insight and understanding of God, which we may not gain from other human beings, simply because animals usually have an untainted view of life. That view may become quite tainted if they have been abused or neglected, but not necessarily. Jenny has not lost her gentleness to humans, even after enduring a very difficult beginning to her life.

Animals, especially dogs (well, cats too), respond to us in ways that are not filtered and without prejudice. They will let you know if you're doing the right thing by them or not, and they will not worry about your feelings or consider your mood when they communicate that information. In fact, every living thing communicates in a fashion. Plants let you know if they need water by limping or beginning to fall over, and if you do nothing to fix them, the plants will die. I have killed many plants in my life, so I know how it works.

Animals will do more, as far as their communication skills, for they are of a higher intelligence than plants. Not always, but that's true of some humans I have encountered as well. The everyday animals who live with us and give us great joy as they romp in the living room with the kids or play games with a ball of yarn or a stick are the ones of whom I speak. I've even had fish who could recognize me when I walked into a room. I was the one who fed them, so when they saw me, and only me, they would swim to the top of the tank, awaiting whatever delicious treat I was about to drop into the tank. I often messed with them and would walk in and out of the room just to watch them go up and down in the tank, but then I realized they were just messing with me.

This book is about an animal who is living beyond what is expected of most animals. It is not only about the dog Jenny but also about how God used her situation and her history to show me something of Him.

She is truly a very special and unique dog. I know that everyone feels that way about their dog, and that's good, for dogs are, or at least may be, one of the greatest friends in a person's life.

I suffer from PTSD and high blood pressure. And Jenny alerts me to both of these things, and so she is designated as a service animal. She has a gentle spirit and loves to visit people. Most owners of service animals ask that the dog be left alone—no eye contact, no touching. I never mind when someone greets Jenny, for she is not disturbed in her work by greeting strangers. I always recommend that people ask the owner if it's OK to pet when approaching someone else's animal, whether that animal is a service animal or not. To interrupt a working animal is disrespectful, to say the least, but it may cause serious harm to an owner who needs the services of that particular animal.

Jenny is so much more than that, though. Because of the PTSD, I can become emotional, and it can happen at lightning speed. Jenny, because she is always nearby, seems to anticipate when I am about to have an emotional event. She will come to me and just park herself in a sitting position and begin a long, deep stare directly at my eyes. This also happens when I'm eating, but I have never had a PTSD episode during dinner. If my blood pressure is high, she will put her head on my leg. I am amazed at how she learned these things and how quickly she did.

I have a friend with whom I am in a monthly meeting. This man endured four tours in Vietnam. Whenever he is near, Jenny goes to him to just give him a little comfort, breaking all protocols for her job but fulfilling the protocols for her ministry. She just knows that he has pain that lives there, and she has a desire—no, a calling—to heal pain, wherever it may be found.

I wrote this book not to glorify my dog, even though she is a dear friend and a wonderful and amazing dog, but to glorify God and to help others see the wonder in all God's creation. He has given each of us gifts—many gifts. And if we are able to slow down our lives enough to look around—or, as Jenny puts it, "sniff things out"—and enjoy the sights and sounds and smells and tastes of this wonderful creation, we will certainly be happier. I hope this book will help you do that and, somehow, help you connect with God in a special way, a way in which you have never before been able to do. It may take a bit more time to do so, but we will enjoy the journey so very much more. Let me introduce you to my friend.

CHAPTER ONE

You Have Not Chosen Me

INTANGIBLES CAN CAUSE confusion and frustration, and they often bring more questions than answers. Things you cannot see, touch, hear, taste, or smell, and are thought of in the abstract, are just like that. So it is that when we seek the intangible, we must not open our eyes wider, shush the noises nearby, or even cleanse our palate. We must make our other senses—our spiritual senses—more attuned to what is nearby. When we are able to do this, and it comes only by repetitive usage, then we will discover that we will inevitably find God. He is at the end of every road, inside every tree, and in each sunset. And He is not only in *these* things but He is within each pain we feel, each tear we shed, as well as in each smile we smile and each laugh we may squeal and each second that moves ever so slowly past us.

I semiretired in July of 2014. As I drew near to retirement, I decided that I wanted to be able to have someone nearby to listen to my bad jokes and not groan or think less of me. And I wanted to have a friend whose presence I would enjoy and with whom I could share both the frustrations I possessed and the pain I had collected throughout my years. I was looking for a counselor who would not speak or share his or her thoughts but would be a willing listener to all my complaints and wisdom (or lack thereof).

I have always been a dog guy, but I had not owned a dog for quite a long time because my job as a full-time Salvation Army pastor required me to travel too often to allow me to be a good owner. I had my sights set on adopting a Doberman pinscher puppy from a reputable breeder. I fell in love with the breed when I had a blue-and-rust Dobie named Eva, pronounced as Afa (Blue Mistress Eva Braun on her papers). She was a loving and gentle dog who loved people. It was during the time that she was in my life when I came to the knowledge of the Lord. In fact, as I fell to my face praying to God for forgiveness for my sins on my living room floor, Eva lie beside me and dutifully held herself in a praying position for the two hours I wept before the throne of God. Coming to the Lord for the first time with my best friend beside me was a great experience.

So it is not really surprising that I wanted to have a buddy to pal around with me as I headed into this stage of my life. The desire to have a friend with fur was certainly something intangible, something I could not explain. But in this desire, I felt more than a need to just have someone with whom to hang out. From working so many disasters in my life and seeing so many people in dire straits, I have been diagnosed with PTSD. I used to think that it was a strange diagnosis, one developed so some folks would have an excuse to get money out of the government. Until it happened to me. What I have discovered is that whenever someone sees something they should not see in the normal course of events in their life, it may cause a little damage to the psyche. My first disaster while working with The Salvation Army was the attacks on our country on 9/11/2001. The tent in which I worked was only fifty feet from the pit, situated directly on the West Side Highway. Daily I would walk over and watch the men and machines slowly remove the debris from that awful pit, and daily I would watch, listen, and smell as bodies of the fallen, the murdered, were removed, ever so slowly and cautiously and with great respect. But it left my heart stunned. Although it wasn't war, it was the aftermath of war. As I spoke with firefighters, law enforcement, construction workers, and others, there entered, at some point, some dark side of me that would never forget that place.

Many, many disasters later, and I have seen much more. I love being there for others—to assist them with whatever they may need in order to bring their lives a sense of normalcy. It is important. And God has blessed me with the training, the ability, and the heart to serve others. I am certainly blessed beyond what I deserve.

It was in May of 2014, as I drew nearer to my semiretirement date, that the desire increased greatly to have a furry friend; and I was having little luck finding a breeder who was nearby. So I thought to myself, *Self, shucks* (that is how I speak to myself), *why limit yourself to a breeder? Perhaps one of the shelters in town may have a Doberman puppy or young dog that would fit the bill* (or something like that). So one day, while I was driving by a shelter called Pet Allies, a no-kill shelter in my home of

Show Low, Arizona, I thought I would just drop in to see if there were any there. As I came through the door, there she was, in a metal crate. She alerted to me and stood, with tail wagging at an amazing speed. And that was no small feat, for her tail was nearly the size of her leg. She was panting heavily and focused on me. I could read in her eyes that she really wanted to leave that place, and she was pleading, putting forth her best performance. I wasn't sure if I was the only one with whom she showed this side, but there was no doubt she meant it.

I smiled at both her enthusiasm and her apparent joy and inquired as to the availability of a Doberman. The wagging body in the crate never lost focus. The lady at the counter saw the intentional communication that was present between the dog and me and asked a series of questions about why I wanted a dog. Having passed the initial questioning, she told me there were no Dobermans available, not even a mix. The wagging mass in the crate looked at me intensely, no slowing in the movement of her body language. She was screaming, "Take me with you!"

I asked the lady, "What's the story on that one?" I pointed with my thumb, trying not to act too enthusiastic. I thought perhaps the price would shoot up if I had an overzealous attitude.

"Oh, that's Jenny... (Frankly, her attitude is more of a Jenni, with an i No offense to the Jennis out there. It's strictly complimentary.) "Jenny is a pretty special dog. But she has very bad separation anxiety, so I've been taking her home with me at night. She doesn't like to be alone at all."

All I could say was, "Uhhnnnhh." I was not quite sure what that meant, but there stood Jenny, who had gotten herself out of the crate yet remained next to it, looking at me hopefully, so hopeful that her entire body was still wagging. And then I saw it. She winked at me. I did a double take, but I was sure she winked at me. I motioned to her, and she immediately came over to me. And in a very kind and gentle way, she nuzzled her nose into my hand. Tail still moving at full speed, she appeared to be telling me "OK, let's go!"

I was being adopted by this creature who, a scant few minutes before, had no idea who I was. This was the first thing she taught me about Jesus: "You have not chosen me, but I have chosen you." I called my wife. She wanted to meet this creature with whom I wanted to form a relationship, to have as a friend. I could tell by the slowness of the response to my invitation that she was less than enthusiastic, putting the meeting off until the next day. But that was OK, for it gave me time to prepare a presentation, which I did.

Jenny's parentage is questionable. She is, what is called in these parts, a rez dog. She was born on the White Mountain Apache reservation to surely a boxer and perhaps a Belgian shepherd. I have had several people tell me that for sure she is this or she is absolutely that. From some of the responses, I think she may be a giraffe/Chihuahua cross. My wife insists she is a boxer/rhinoceros cross. When I googled *cross boxer and Belgian shepherd* and saw the images, I found one that was an exact match. Knowing that everything you find on the Internet is true, Jenny is a cross between a boxer and a Belgian shepherd. Her eyes look like they have a thick line of mascara and very nicely shaped eyebrows. I knew when my wife, Tina, met her, she would fall in love too.

I was right. The next morning, when Tina came to meet Jenny, they were instant friends. I began the paperwork to adopt Jenny. During the process, I discovered a bit more of Jenny's history. She had been adopted before but returned after a short time because she shed a lot. For all of you who may be considering adopting a dog, they shed. Some of them shed a lot. If you don't like hair, get a fish. Or perhaps a Mexican hairless. They are so cute. OK. You got me. I am being sarcastic.

The shelter tried everything, including shaving her. I know that sounds a bit ridiculous, but I guess sometimes it works. Luckily for me, it didn't. She spent over a year in the shelter because no one wants a dog that looks like that. But during her time in the shelter, she had been micro chipped and spayed. So glad for that. When everything was in order, we left for home.

When Jenny got in my truck, she had no hesitation at all. She jumped right up into the back seat of my truck and immediately did what all dogs do, smelled what was up. She stood in the back seat just looking out the window. I started up the truck, and she continued to look out; so I rolled the window down enough so she could get her head out the window. She continued to just stand there, so I started to drive. She looked at me for a few moments, as if to size me up, and then turned and looked back out the window. But as soon as I pulled out onto the highway, she placed her two front paws up on the armrest on the door, stood up as tall as she could, and put her head out the window. I looked back over my right shoulder and saw her with her eyes closed, and with the wind blowing in her face, she looked like she was in heaven. She still does this every time we drive somewhere. And always with that expression of supreme joy on her face—sometimes with her mouth open just a bit, sometimes closed. I believe she has learned through her experiences that, sometimes, the journey is not always comfortable, and sometimes, it is difficult. But when you are free to have the wind in your face, do so with great enthusiasm.

That's the second thing she taught me about Jesus: abandon all caution and enjoy the journey. God is giving you a great but simple gift of moving air, and it is good to take each moment like the one you are in, moments that are filled with joy and new smells—enjoy them with all you have. Savor the good. Forget the bad and difficult. It is better to let the past be past.

I have no idea of Jenny's past. From knowing a bit of her history, I know that it has been difficult. Such beginnings are always difficult. But the difference is that she has not let her past shape who she is. And neither should we. We may have come from a place of sadness, a place of pain, a place of loss, a place of abuse, or a place of abandonment. Although all these places are not the places we would choose to be, they may be places where we have, by our own choices, put ourselves. That, of course, is not always the case, but for most adults, we live where our choices have taken us. Sometimes we are abandoned by those who we thought we could trust or have been betrayed by those we loved. Perhaps we were adopted and then returned because we didn't meet the requirements of the adoptive parent. There are absolutely no guidelines for pain and loss, but I do know there is One who will never leave you, who will never betray you or cause you pain.

He may not prevent pain from happening, but His promise is to stay with us as we suffer. It may be that as we travel through difficulties that cause suffering, we will learn something in the midst of the pain. Please know this, though. We cannot discover anything unless we learn to enjoy each moment, to praise God for both the good and the bad. No one wants to suffer, but all of us will—sometimes physically, sometimes mentally, sometimes spiritually. But if our relationship with our Maker is good, one of depending upon Him to guide, comfort, teach, and sustain us through the tough times, we will be made stronger and will learn to trust God, even when it seems like we shouldn't.

Jenny has suffered much in her short life, but she has shown me that the love that comes when you find that forever home is worth the suffering and worth the wait. Her loyalty to me because I freed her from that crate, from a life held in bondage, made her instantly devoted to me. We are both better off because of what we have found in the company of each other.

When we come to the understanding that Jesus has done the same for us—freed us from our bondage, taken us from a place of suffering, and willingly brought us into our forever home—it only stands to reason that we should have a display of loyalty to Him that emulates the loyalty Jenny has shown me. We have so little time on this earth and in this place. We should find the One who has promised us that He will never leave us or forsake us and go home with Him. He will roll the window down and let us breathe in the sweet smell of freedom as He drives us down that highway. It is a remarkable sensation.

If Jenny had thumbs, I would let her drive, and I would sit in the back and stick my head out the window just so I could feel the sensation she does. It must be quite remarkable, for she certainly has the most amazing expression of joy on her face when she does it. I want that expression plastered all over my face as well.

DAVID ROSS SHERMAN

CHAPTER TWO

It's Tough to Obey

UPON ARRIVAL AT her new home, Jenny jumped out of the car and began to smell everything in sight. I gave her some time to smell things out and saw that she could detect the smell of the evil darkness of cat. We had two that were strictly outdoor cats who were abandoned by a moving neighbor, and we have fed them for years. After showing her where the cats hung out, or actually her showing me, I invited her inside. She became quite excited running from room to room and smelling the smells of her new home. She didn't know it was a forever home yet, but I did.

She rolled on her back in an attempt to get that smell all over her, and she performed, as promised, the shadow dance. This was a very insecure animal. My repeated question, though, what did they do to you? went unanswered. She began to follow me wherever I walked, never more than a few feet away. She still does. I believe that all dogs should be trained—to whatever extent it is possible to train them. Let's face it, some are smarter than others. I was basing my opinion of Jenny's intelligence on her obviously wise choice to pick me. But even more than that, I am a believer that God does grant us a more-than-the-occasional desire of our heart, and whether He granted her desire or mine, I knew that we were destined for a great relationship. And then I saw it.

Stubbornness—the desire to *not* do what someone else wants you to do just because they want you to do it. At least that's what it looks like. And sometimes that's good because it denotes tenacity and perseverance, but nearly always if something has a good side, there is a difficult side as well. The reason I could spot it so easily in Jenny is because it is in me, in magnificently great quantity. I am a stubborn man. I know it. My wife is particularly well versed in this attribute of mine. God knows it. But with God, it has put a strain sometimes on our relationship. But God has all the power, and I certainly know that, so I always, sometimes after a great struggle, acquiesce. What can I do? Struggle with God? I discovered a long time ago that that isn't wise.

It is not pretty when I disobey, and when I learn to surrender early in the battle, I achieve victory, pleasing my Father. Jenny knows the commands. She knows the words. She knows the hand gestures. Someone had worked with her before I ever met her, for she certainly understood some basic instructions. You know, *sit, down, stay.* But her version was often a bit different than my version, and as of this writing, it still is. And then there's the outright disobedience. We live in a neighborhood of many dogs. Perfect.

This gives dog owners the opportunity to teach their dog to ignore other dogs. Unless said dog is a puppy. Dogs love to greet one another. Their version of a friendly hug is sometimes varied but usually involves sniffing around the part that generates the most smells. Identification is important in their society. Jenny is really good at this, and her desire is to discover all the varied aromas of all the doggie neighbors. But it isn't mine.

I am attempting to teach her that the most pleasant aroma she can ever smell is mine. It's a hard sell. There are so many aromas, and she doesn't care if they are pleasant or not so much. But each one tells a story to her, and she loves every story. When the allure of something new pulls her toward it, I usually resent it, because in some twisted way, it seems as though she is rejecting me for whatever it is that has drawn her. I am so glad that God doesn't do that with me. I am often distracted from His pleasing aroma. And what I usually find myself doing is searching for a better version of His aroma, which is impossible, instead of trying to make myself a pleasant aroma to Him.

To God, the most pleasant aroma we can offer is the aroma of Him through us. That's what is meant in Hosea 6:6 when He says,

> *For I desire mercy and not sacrifice, And the knowledge of God more than burnt offerings.*

Mercy is one of God's greatest attributes. We would be toast without it. It is the ultimate in obedience. Forgive and you shall be forgiven. As Jenny slowly comes to the knowledge that I am only concerned about her welfare and that my desire is always for her and to never cause her harm, she is learning to obey. That is the ultimate in trust after all, to obey the voice of the One who has given you hope. If we fail in this, we will fail completely. We must show that we are in the process of growing—by putting a bit more time between repeating the same sins, by showing a bit more love to our neighbors, by spending a little more time in both communication with God and gaining knowledge of God. These are the ways we show ourselves approved to God.

When Jenny does anything in obedience, I reward her by letting her know that she did well—nothing else. I occasionally engage in reward training but only occasionally. It sometimes sets an animal up for misinterpreting the reasons for being obedient, which should be simply pleasing her master. For me to be pleasing to my Master, I too must be obedient. And I should need no reward to accomplish it. The knowledge that I have pleased my Master should be all the reward I need. She taught me that. If it's good enough for Jenny, it's good enough for me.

Jenny doesn't leap all over, doing the happy dance in order for me to understand that she is appreciative of my atta girls but I also understand that she needs them in order to feel complete. Do you not think that God understands that as well? Our rewards for obedience here may not be felt in ways our physical bodies can garner the most satisfaction, but we should bask in the knowledge that obedience to God will always offer spiritual rewards. And those rewards are more of God's presence and more knowledge of Him. Not always, though. Remember, Jesus said this in Matthew 7:7–11:

> Ask, and it will be given to you; seek, and you will find; knock, and it will be opened to you. 8 For everyone who asks receives, and he who seeks finds, and to him who knocks it will be opened. 9 Or what man is there among you who, if his son asks for bread, will give him a stone? 10 Or if he asks for a fish, will he give him a serpent? 11 If you then, being evil, know how to give good gifts to your children, how much more will your Father who is in heaven give good things to those who ask Him!

Of course, even if we are not seeking Him as we should, God's presence and God's great love are never removed because of our actions, and I know this to be true. We may remove ourselves from His presence, but He will never leave us. Some think we are punished for disobedience by suffering, and I know that is not true because some of the most loving and godly people I know are those who suffer great and often quite painful difficulties. It is heartbreaking to see people who are so in love with God suffer so badly, yet the mark of a true believer is one who suffers well and praises Him throughout the turmoil of his suffering. Suffering is growth.

Jenny taught me that as well. Suffering is just a part of life, but don't ever, and I mean ever, let it destroy your joy. I don't mean happiness. I mean your ability to grow in your relationship with God even while, perhaps *especially* while, you are suffering greatly. If you are going to suffer anyway, doesn't it make sense to get close to the One who has promised to go through this pain with you?

I lean on God when I can't figure things out or when I am in pain. That is how it should be. But our obedience is never the determining factor of how we stand in God's presence or the reason we receive His gifts and rewards. We should do His will simply because He is God and we aren't. He never asks us to do something out of the bounds of His love, so we need not worry that evil has somehow inhabited His will and He will require evil of us. Jenny knows as well that I would never ask her to do something that is counter to my ultimate care for her or love for my fellow humans, but she stands ready to defend me against evil should it appear. What a great thing that is. Oh, that we were that way when it came to God.

If only we can gather some basic understanding about God. He never has anything but the best in mind for his children—the absolute best. He never desires that we have evil circumstances in our lives, but He does allow us to determine our own path. All the choices I have ever made have led me to where I am today. There has been both evil and good in my life, but the times that were lived within the limits of goodness are the times of greatest joy. Even Jenny gets that concept. She knows that if she is obedient, she lives within my blessing, but if she walks out of those bounds, she has made a choice to do so and will pay the consequences of that action. Please don't think that I will strike her, but the consequences will be harsher voice and body language that shows my disappointment. But it is possible, I suppose, that she could stray so far from my sight that harm could come to her. I don't think that will happen, but it is possible. So it is with God. It is possible, and in fact, it's not very difficult, to walk away from God so far that

His protection fails us. Free will can be a booger. Why would we expect God's blessings when we live in disobedience to His will for us? We certainly want all His blessings but often have difficulty in being obedient to His will. Jenny can't have it both ways—neither can I and neither can you.

What may be most difficult for us to answer though—when the time comes to answer—is, why didn't you seek to obey? If we fail while at least seeking after obedience, we will have succeeded. Because we are promised that if we seek Him, we will find Him. If we find Him, we will be changed. If there is no change, then we have found something else because the presence of God—near us, close to us, even within us—will change us. There can be no other outcome. If that change doesn't happen, then you have not yet discovered God. But never fret, for He has promised that if you seek Him, you will find Him—if you seek Him with all your heart.

Deuteronomy 4:29

> *But from there you will seek the Lord your God, and you will find Him if you seek Him with all your heart and with all your soul.*

When Jenny was lost and alone, living within the confines of a cage for over a year, somehow she managed to maintain her joy, believing that one day she would find a home that would allow her to maximize her talents of love and mercy and eventually (I hope) obedience. All we can do is hope for the same. When that day happens, both Master and servant will smile at one another but more as a child to his Father than a servant to his master.

DAVID ROSS SHERMAN

CHAPTER THREE

I'm Not Going Anywhere without You

I TAKE A while to wake up. The time for this activity has increased exponentially as I get older. I need some time and some good, strong coffee. Jenny does not have a very difficult job during the day, so she gets a lot of sleep—a lot of sleep. Dogs are good that way, but there are, for every dog, different types of sleep. I am pretty sure they get into REM sleep just because you can see dogs dreaming. When any animal is in one of those really deep sleeps, it can be quite amusing if you need them to move rapidly for any reason. I have had many laughs at the expense of some unwary animals by simply waking them too quickly. Sorry. I apologize to those whom I may have caused undue anxiety.

Jenny is no exception. She usually needs a moment to arrive at a state of excitement—that is, unless she hears the word *outside*. I do believe it is her favorite word. I have seen her jump into a standing position from a seemingly intense sleep when I ask, "Do you want to go outside?"

She may not know what we are going to do, specifically, but to her, it doesn't matter, because whatever it is, it is in her favorite place. Anything that happens there is OK. Snowing? No problem. Raining? I don't care. Outside...it is what's happening in her world. She does perform a bit of a ritual when she steps outside. She will walk the couple of feet to the descending stairs and put her front paws on the first step down while staying seated on the porch. If I don't step out onto the porch, she will proceed no farther. She will just sit there. If I step out onto the porch, she will run anywhere in the yard, even out of my sight, without any reservation. But if she hears the door open and shut, she will return to her place at the top of the stairs because she knows I have gone back inside.

We are able to do a similar thing with God, or perhaps I should say, we should. God is consistently putting opportunities before us, but when the door opens a little bit, even a very tiny little crack, we often see it as a sign that we should burst out the door and do whatever it is we had in mind to do. Sometimes it works out, but most of the time, this approach will only bring us pain and grief. Most of us are very poor at waiting on Him to lead or give us a plan. We rarely wait and often run ahead without making sure He is there watching, guiding, and protecting.

Jenny waits on me because she knows two things: I will protect her and it is her duty to let me know if there's anything of which I should beware. God doesn't need us to make Him aware, but He most certainly will protect us if we stand under His protection and guidance. Too often, though, we wander off without even considering where we are going. We don't wait for Him to step out behind us and give us the nod to proceed, and so we race into the unknown without considering Him at all. Whether you know it or not, that is sin. It is the sin of pride. And God promises nothing while we are in a state of sin. I am not saying you will burn in hell for eternity, but operating beyond the protection of the only One who is able to protect you in the world of the spirit is very foolish.

God is more than willing to lead us, but we must be willing to be led. Jenny climbed a chain-link fence the very first day I had her and wandered just beyond my ability to protect her. When I saw her in the vacant lot next door, I called her name and shouted, "You can get hurt over there. What are you doing? Come back over here now." She ran back over to where she had climbed the fence, and I watched in amazement as she climbed it again, returning to her yard. I was quite impressed at her ability to climb up and over a chain-link fence. And I was also impressed at her understanding of what I wanted her to do. We too are able to return to the Lord the same way we left—that is, if we are able. Sometimes we wander too far off and find it extremely difficult to come back the same way, and we become lost. Being lost can be quite scary.

I wonder if God is also impressed and amazed when we figure out the way back. Sometimes He needs to go to some extraordinary means to make us understand, and even though He does that, some still will not respond, and they stay in that lost state.

When I saw that Jenny had a yearning to explore her new digs, I simply put a leash on her and showed her the neighborhood. She never tried to go exploring on her own again. We should be the same way when we return home. At some point, we may go beyond God's protection for too far and too long a time and find ourselves in great difficulties, but He is always willing to show us where we are if we are willing to submit to His divine influence. That is grace. No, really. That *is* grace.

The word in Greek is *charis*. It means "graciousness (as gratifying), of manner or act (abstract or concrete; literal, figurative or spiritual; especially the divine influence upon the heart, and its reflection in the life; including gratitude)."[1]

When we act like God—when we reflect His actions, and when we do things as He would do them—that is grace. When we emulate the actions of our Savior, that is grace. It is free. But we make the choice to do it. God will continue showing us the proper way to insert His attributes by continually placing us in situations where His attributes will be necessary. If we are standing on the porch, awaiting His guidance, we will always be successful. If we choose to leave His protection, we also usually leave His grace, which is a big mistake.

Jenny shows her readiness to go by putting herself in the position to go. Then she awaits my voice or my signal to release her to go. Part of that is fear of the unknown, perhaps, but I think it is more an attempt to please her master. If we desire to please our Master as well, we will most certainly await His voice that gives us the signal to move ahead.

After Jenny had been with me for over a year, we were playing hide-and-go-seek in the driveway. It was a very raucous game, and we had been going at it for a while when she heard the thundering sound of a neighbor's truck who lives a couple of blocks away. It must have sounded like the growl of a vicious animal to her. She stopped our game and ran into the street in hopes of catching the elusive truck and bringing it home to me for a prize (or at least, that's how I imagined it). I shouted her name but to no avail. On the second try, my volume escalated to

---

[1]   Biblesoft's New Exhaustive Strong's Numbers and Concordance with Expanded Greek-Hebrew Dictionary. Copyright © 1994, 2003, 2006. Biblesoft Inc. and International Bible Translators Inc.

just below the sound barrier, and she halted in her tracks and returned immediately to me. She had no idea what could have happened, and all she knew was that she was going to catch that irritating truck. She completely forgot where she was, what she was doing, and with whom she was doing it. "Catch the truck. Must catch truck!" But what stopped her was my voice. When we heed the voice of our Father and stop what we are doing, he blesses us and brings us back into His presence.

Charging ahead without the benefit of God's protection, God's guidance, and God's blessing is operating without the wisdom of God. I know because I have done it. And I have done it far too often. Sometimes it worked out but not usually. It is much better to prepare yourself spiritually by prayer, meditation, and seeking His wisdom before you proceed with any plan on which you have set your heart. This way, you operate within the bounds of His grace. You have placed yourself in a position of readiness; you are awaiting His command to proceed, and when that command comes, you may jump at the opportunity He shows you because you have prepared. You are ready.

Jenny had to learn that I am her safety; I am her guide. She no longer runs into the street to chase the growling vehicles that pass by, but she will run into the fenced portion of the yard and bark at them as they pass and make them understand that when they growl as they roll down the road, they can expect trouble from the self-appointed guardian of the street.

Do yourself a favor. Be ready to jump only when He gives you the OK to do so, even if you have prepared. You will be glad you did.

CHAPTER FOUR

I Got Joy, Joy, Joy, Joy

I HAVE MET people who seem defeated. I just got off the phone with one. He is convinced that God has abandoned him. He is dying. This is a man I have known for nine years. He spent thirty-one years in the military. A year and a half ago, he found his wife in the driveway, having fallen out of her wheelchair. She was dead. As you might imagine, he was devastated. About seven months later, he was diagnosed with colon cancer. He is dying. He tells me that he asked God to heal him, and God has not. He believes that God has abandoned him because he is dying.

I told him that if everyone who asked was healed, not too many would die for nearly everyone asks. The valley of the shadow of death is not an easy path, yet we will all experience it. It is made easier and becomes a fearless path if we are able to keep ourselves aware of the presence of God. David stated in Psalm 23 that even though he walks through the valley of the shadow of death, he will fear no evil for God is with him. His presence brings both peace and joy to any situation. It is very difficult indeed to find joy in my friend's situation, perhaps in most of his life. He was sexually abused as a child by the very one who was supposed to protect him. He believes God abandoned him then as well. I have attempted, but failed thus far, to make my friend understand that dying isn't the worst thing that can happen to someone. I believe that people who think that are so afraid of death that they abandon reason and live in the pain of their fear.

Jenny spent over a year in a cage that was about eight feet long and four feet wide, with a metal bowl with water and a little blanket on which to lie that covered a small part of the concrete floor. I can almost guarantee there were days she would have preferred death. I am pretty sure I would have. But she owns a particular joy that is difficult to describe. As I said before, she has not allowed her past to shape who she is. Although it has not been easy, she is grateful for the goodness that has now overtaken her life. She beams with joy and greets every person she meets with that sincere tail waggin', hard pantin' that personifies a joy that is never mistaken for anything else.

She acts as though she knows the command of the Lord.

After the children of Israel left Babylon and Nehemiah had begun to act as governor in Jerusalem, they had a day where the law was read in the town square, apparently around a giant water feature in the middle of town. Ezra the priest tried to quiet everyone down because they began to weep and wail and mourn at hearing the law. Remember, seventy years were spent in slavery in Babylon. They were mourning for time lost. Ezra spoke these words found in Nehemiah 8:10:

> *Then he said to them, "Go your way, eat the fat, drink the sweet, and send portions to those for whom nothing is prepared; for this day is holy to our Lord. Do not sorrow, for the joy of the Lord is your strength.*

I find it amazing (not surprising) that the joy of the Lord is where we may find strength. Jenny figured that out in her "doggieness" better than most humans who possess the ability to reason and think are able to do. When she left the coldness and inhospitality of the cage, she welcomed the warmth and hospitality of our home. She never looked back. She never let her memory of the cage obscure the joy she has for her new situation. If we are able to do the same, we can pass through our lives as new creations, freed from the past, forever.

My friend will die as we all will. Lazarus was raised from the dead but even Lazarus died eventually. My friend has suffered extreme pain in his years, as many have. The suffering he has endured is not the worst ever suffered, nor was his life the most joyous ever lived. I have shown him scriptures that speak of owning joy in the midst of suffering and reminded him that even Jesus suffered. He is God and the only One who should have been exempt from suffering. All of us suffer, but the author of Hebrews reminds us of why Jesus suffered in Hebrews 12:1–2:

> *Therefore we also, since we are surrounded by so great a cloud of witnesses, let us lay aside every weight, and the sin which so easily ensnares us, and let us run with endurance*

*the race that is set before us, looking unto Jesus, the author and finisher of our faith, **who for the joy that was set before Him** endured the cross, despising the shame, and has sat down at the right hand of the throne of God.*

What an amazing thing joy is and can be in the life of every single person who is suffering. In my first book, *Learning to Agalliao*, I detail a specific type of joy that lives in the midst of tragedy and pain. Jesus endured suffering because He knew of the joy that would outlive His situation. This kind of joy lives in hope, for hope understands that pain is temporary. Yet joy, if lived in a manner prescribed by God, is eternal. If our goal is being with Christ and sharing eternity with those who, like me, don't deserve the benefit of that relationship, then we should be able to endure this temporary situation, no matter what that situation entails. It is never easy, but I have never seen or heard any promises from God that give us the promise of freedom from pain and suffering. I do recall one that sounds like a promise made that we will, indeed, suffer.

John 16:33

These things I have spoken to you, that in Me you may have peace. In the world you will have tribulation; but be of good cheer, I have overcome the world.

The joy that outlives our difficult situations and also accompanies us through those same situations is the joy that brings peace. Since Jesus told us that He has overcome the world, it seems to me that He is the only place where such joy can be found in this world. Of course, Jenny doesn't and can't know Jesus, so she exhibits the joy, which lives in her soul, only because God has instilled such joy in innocence. That is why so many animals seem to possess an unexplainable joy. We are not innocent, so we must search for His joy. But once again, He promised that if we seek, we will find it. Jenny, along with so many other animals, shows us what that joy should look like. I think that is why so many people are attracted to animals, even more than humans.

Joy is a found thing. You must be looking. In my own life, I have discovered that if you are looking, you will be able to discover joy in every situation. It may not be always lying in the path you are walking, but if, while on that path—be it a path of pain, loneliness, suffering, or any other difficult thing—it is there, just off that difficult path. And as far as I can tell, it is always found in the same place. That place is in the arms of Jesus.

There may be joyous events that happen in life that bring us some time of happiness, but I think that happiness and joy are two very different things. Happiness is an emotion that is fleeting and, because it is fleeting, will never be able to replace the deep joy found in the soul of the one who has an abiding relationship with God. Happiness is a result of an event. Joy lives in someone in spite of all events that may happen and never depends on an event to be manifested in someone's life. It just exists and is the basis for all their actions.

Now don't get me wrong. If you own joy in your life, it does not mean you won't ever have anger or sadness or any other of the ten million emotions that accompany life. But it does mean that after some negative emotion has reared its ugly head, and in whatever way that has happened, joy will overtake and bring you back to a place where you can quickly be restored to a better place. Joy owns you.

Jenny is an absolutely perfect personification (can I use that word when speaking of an animal?) of that. I have seen her (caught her or observed her) doing something she was not supposed to be doing, and when I raised my voice to stop her, she would immediately cease and lower her head as though she had been found stealing food off the alpha's plate. Her body language is always so telltale and gives away her negative emotions immediately. But within a matter of a few seconds, her joy returns. The joy that lives in her heart is the joy that shows up in all she does. And if joy lives in your heart, the same will be true.

Of course, it may take a bit longer for most people who have joy living deep within their souls to have that joy resurface when some dark evil hits them hard. That is due to the fact that humans tend toward actually desiring some sort of suffering or, at least, reliving it for others. We love to speak of the difficulties we endure. That is why people love to speak of the aches and pains they have. We love having someone to empathize with us and, even better, to sympathize with us. Have you ever listened to a couple of people discussing their latest medical problems? It can be like a tennis match of who is actually worse off. It almost sounds like they are finding some joy in their pain, but I can't quite understand how that works. I would rather find my joy by focusing on some positive things.

Jesus said this about joy returning after pain was experienced:

John 16:21–22

> *A woman, when she is in labor, has sorrow because her hour has come; but as soon as she has given birth to the child, she no longer remembers the anguish, for joy that a human being has been born into the world. Therefore you now have sorrow; but I will see you again and your heart will rejoice, and your joy no one will take from you.*

If we are focused on Christ and the good things that are to come when we embrace Him with all the strength we have, when we seek Him with all our heart and all our strength, then our joy will be never ending, for in every desperate situation, we will have hope. In Jenny, hope springs eternal simply because she finds so much joy in her life. I don't know what the cage was like for her, but I do know that she had never allowed the cage to define her. One of the workers at the shelter from which I adopted Jenny told me that many days they would come in and find her hanging from the very top of the chain-link fence gate. She would climb up there and just hang out, looking around and enjoying things.

Her joy is unmistakable. In fact, I took her the other night to a regular Friday night gathering in the town in which I live. Some Christian musicians get together and play and just get lost in worshipping the Lord. There are usually only a few people there, and last Friday was no different. Jenny made her way around the room and was just being her joyful self, attempting to make sure everyone knew that if they needed a lift, she would be glad to supply it. One of the ladies turned to me and said, "That is the most joyful animal I have ever seen!" I just smiled at her as I watched Jenny prance around the room and repeated, as I so often do, "I know. She has the joy of the Lord."

I just wish everyone could have such joy. What a really wonderful world this would be.

CHAPTER FIVE

I Will Persevere

M OST OF US who have something to do sometimes struggle with getting it done. It is nothing we should be ashamed, but it is true. And then there are some who never fail, and it seems that they never even have to try to succeed. But were we able to place ourselves in the position of having to know their entire story, seeing each time those kinds of people had attempted and then failed, we would indeed change our thoughts regarding how these people have come to know success. That is, in part, due to the fact that success has many measures, and the thing that controls the measure we utilize is a combination of our present and our past. If we have had a difficult past, our success, or at least the measure we use for measuring success, will most certainly be affected, but whether that effect is negative or positive is all about love being present in the present.

Are you now thoroughly confused? Let me attempt to clarify.

Love may not have ever before shown up in anyone's life, but the moment it does, that person's perspective becomes somehow different, somehow gentler, and hopefully, somehow wiser. That is what the *Phantom of the Opera* and *Beauty and the Beast* were all about. That is what the Bible is all about. Wisdom is about these two things as well—our past and our present. All these interlocking jigsaw pieces make a life—a life that is kept by the hand of God. For it is God who not only initiates life but sustains it. It is God who allows all things to exist. And not only that, He is also in control of the degree to which that soul—that physical embodiment of the Lord—is gifted and nurtured. And all the talents and gifts given from the hand of God to each and every person who lives are matured, grown, expanded, maximized, and utilized by merely the presence of the combination of love and perseverance.

And to take the description of this combination just one step further, it is the combination of *God's* love and *our* perseverance that enables us to form a measure of success that can be assessed in no other way than through God's eyes and our perception. God gives everyone gifts. Everyone. The children of God, once they know and understand that God really loves them, will do everything possible to identify their talents and then grow them and use those very same talents for the glory of God. And I don't mean that every Christian is a singer. As a matter of fact, I *know* that to be true. You may own a talent that allows you to be organized and very efficient, or perhaps you are good at being friendly. Your talent may be that you are able to show courage in the face of danger, defeat, and desperation. But no matter your talent, rest assured that unless you possess and are aware of God's love and you persevere to develop the talent God gave you, it will not develop past the very basic thing it is when you first discovered it. And that is not where God desires you to be. Growth is a requirement of joy for it enables us to stop, listen, and learn rather than speak and act without thought, for maturity always enables us to receive the wisdom of God before we act.

Jenny grew up on the streets, and it was a tough place to be. Life expectancy for a rezdog is relatively short, especially if they are either born in or pushed into the streets or the forest that surrounds most of the White Mountain Apache lands. I really have no idea about the circumstances surrounding her initial appearance in this world. I was just told she was a rez dog. For those who live in these parts, that is as close to a leper as you want to be. It explains much about the way she is with other dogs. Some she tolerates; some she will just go after as if that's the one who killed her mother while she watched. But even with that, Jenny showed me that if you discover love, you can change . . . if only you persevere.

She has gotten better, and I encourage her to mix with other dogs in order to prove to her that not all dogs are mean, and for the most part, once properly sniffed out, Jenny will tolerate them and some have become playmates. But she is ever so cautious. People are the same way, though. We need to make sure when we meet someone that they mean us no harm. But if we grew up on the streets, we may be a bit more cautious than we would be had we never been attacked for just looking like we do. It is doubtful that we would attack because of some aroma that brought to our memory survival of an attack from the past, but then again, who knows what the human heart can do? Until we have trod the same path, we cannot say with any sense of surety that we might not react similarly.

Let us return to the topic of perseverance. All behavior is learned and, most of that, self-taught. We are able to achieve any change required so we might better fit into our environment, one of more socially acceptable behaviors if only we persevere. But we must have first the desire to change. If we would only look to those who have gone before us as examples, we could more easily move into those things we see as so difficult to change. Think of it. It's one less thing to work on during the journey. But we must identify first and then employ perseverance to make it come together. Perseverance is how permanent change is accomplished.

I mentioned in chapter 3 that the first day I brought Jenny home, I saw her in the yard next door after I walked outside and had left her alone for no more than a moment. I had no idea how she arrived there. There was no entrance to that yard from where I last saw her, and she didn't have enough time to get there from going around through the front of our property. I looked at her and simply said, "You can get hurt over there. What are you doing? Come back over here now." As soon as I said that, she just walked over to the chain-link fence and climbed straight up and over the fence. It took some perseverance to learn that trick. Dogs are not natural climbers. But she showed by her ease of accomplishment that there was little effort required and that she had done it many times. It also showed me that she didn't need scolding; she just needed direction. She needed to know that she could stay on her side of the fence and be perfectly safe. After that first day, she has never climbed the fence again. She is now aware that she need not go seeking after other things. All she needs, she will find at home. We humans would do well to learn that one.

The reason we struggle with change, even positive change, is because of our nature and our past. These two things together are like two monsters who are somewhat peaceful and controllable when we take them on individually, but when they show up simultaneously, it can be murder. Jenny grew up on the street. That was her past. It left in her a desire to always be prepared for assault. She also has a pack mentality, which is pretty much in every dog. It is their nature, after all. When both of these things show themselves during some sort of training, she is not going to learn anything. When her street persona shows up while we are working on something, it makes the training difficult. But when she is in street mode because of a dog in the area and pack mentality is present and in the forefront, it is much too much for her to pay attention to anything else. It may express itself in varied ways, but once I get her attention, she comes right back. I just need to get her attention. Even then she may argue with me about it.

We often act the same with God. When we are drawn by the presence of something tempting, something distracting, and something that makes our flesh take notice, we retreat rather quickly to our world before the Lord. It doesn't have to be some temptation, but it could be some action you take that identifies you as still in possession of this worldly quality—be it lust, anger, greed, or something else. It is so very easy to do and can happen in a matter of the blink of an eye. If we have retained any of the former man, it is so very much more difficult to resist those things that promise temporary enjoyment or even a temporary return to the things that once ruled and controlled us. This is impossible to fight, for it is in our nature to run toward the satisfying and the pleasing.

But just as Jenny is able to ignore the temptation that exists if she is focused on me and my direction, if we will only keep our eyes on the Lord, we will not fail to achieve His will in our lives. But we must keep our eyes on Him. Just like the hymn that says, "Keep your eyes upon Jesus, / look full in His wonderful face, / and the things of earth will grow strangely dim in the light of His glory and grace."

We are, of all creatures, unique. We have the ability to think, to speak, to take actions that can change our own situations and attitudes, and to show affection, care, mercy, kindness, and love to others. But with all these wonderful abilities, we seem to have a propensity to constantly be in a state of turmoil and worry and concern. Sometimes, when things happen, when our lives change in negative ways, we often may find that we react negatively and cause undue concern—not only for ourselves but for others, even those for whom we care. This is especially true in those situations over which we have no control.

But if we have a relationship with God, and I am speaking not of a Sunday only or even daily type of relationship with God but one that allows you to seek Him with *all* your heart, all your mind, and all your strength, then it can happen. The prophet Isaiah wrote this in Isaiah 26:3:

You will keep him in perfect peace, Whose mind is stayed on You, Because he trusts in You.

This is really an amazing scripture. The word *perfect* here is really the word *peace*. It is *shalom*. When a word in Hebrew is repeated twice, it puts it in the perfect tense. So it sounds like "shalom, shalom." But look at how this perfect peace comes to be. It is by keeping your mind stayed on God. The word *stayed* is a word that means either "to lean on or to take hold of."

Now please understand something. This cannot be taken lightly. There are two major things that will happen if we keep our minds stayed or fixed on God. And we must take great pains to try and understand this. By keeping your mind on God, first of all, you will not sin. Your mind will be focused on the light so that darkness cannot invade, not even a little bit. It will try, but keeping your mind stayed on Christ prevents any thoughts of evil from entering. Darkness, evil, and wickedness cannot be where the presence of Christ dwells.

The other thing that will happen when your mind is stayed on Christ is that the peace of Christ will come to you. But you must keep your mind stayed on Him. When we think about our situation, all may seem bleak. We may be in pain, or we may be suffering through what is an extreme situation. We may be asking God to take whatever it is that is happening to us away from us and to no avail. And for all our consideration, we cannot understand why we must go through this. All our requests are apparently falling on deaf ears. Nothing is changing.

The world of the present and the world of the past are both constantly there to bring us back from where we are with God. Unless we persevere to keep God in the forefront of our daily walk, we will easily be distracted by the call of the world to draw us. Let's face it, the world has some pretty attractive things. And because we may have needs to fill in so very many different areas of life, it may seem as though these needs could be filled by those things the world offers. But in the end, and I mean the end of our lives here, we will realize that nothing the world has to offer could possibly give us any real satisfaction, for the world can only satisfy temporarily. To conquer the two things (filling our needs and being satisfied) takes two things. It takes the Holy Spirit as well as our dedication to the task. It takes perseverance.

CHAPTER SIX

Overcoming the Pack

SOME DOGS JUST won't wait on you, not even if it will only be a very short wait—a matter of only a minute or two. Some will take advantage of the situation and take a nap and hope that the time spent waiting will be a long time. Jenny will wait a very long time for me to do whatever I need to do as long as she is included in the end of things. In other words, if it means she will be going outside. She will assume the position I call her "prayer" position, with her nose resting on the ground between her two paws. When she prays, she shows extreme patience and will watch me walk around gathering things for the big exit. Her head never rises, but her eyes will follow me as long as I stay within range, head immobile and fixed between those white socks of hers.

Once she sees I am going to make a move for the door, her prayer is answered. We can go outside. Wouldn't it be great if we could just wait until we saw that God is moving before we moved? I spend so much of my time thinking up my plans and then planning out, with great detail, those things I desire to do. I don't always ask God what He thinks, and more often than not, I ignore Him when He does happen to mention something to me that is instructive when it comes to some project—probably not the best plan. God desires that we listen to Him only for our own good. He desires that we wait for Him for our own good.

Every single time I have moved ahead of the Lord in any project or plan, it seems it fails. I have small successes then—blammo!—it's on the floor with me and whatever it was I was doing. I would bet a dime to a doughnut that Jenny has experienced that as well. It beats you up. Prisons can do that to you and damage you, or you can look at it as just something that happens. Not everything in our lives work out the way we would like, yet life goes on until it is over. If we don't forget the past and live for our future, owning joy and love and distributing those qualities to all we meet, then we truly miss out on living our lives to the fullest.

Jenny taught me that. One of the things that amazes me about her is that she was defeated so many times, yet to her, those defeats were only a way to grow in the opposite way of what you might expect. Growing up in a place where fear and suspicion own every day and grow into the night, fear and suspicion should be her attitude. But they are not. She was apprehended for no other reason than being free (that's how she saw it, I am sure) and brought to a place that was block and mortar and fences. High fences that closed the end of an eight-foot-by-four-foot-by-eight-foot-high cinder block cell that contained a soft bed (blanket) on a concrete floor and a water dish. Fear and suspicion should rule her attitude, but they do not. She was adopted and then returned because she shed her hair more than her owner desired. They shaved her. It did not help. They returned her to her four-by-eight cell. Fear and suspicion should be all-encompassing, but they cannot be found in her anywhere. She spent a year in that cage.

Now I have stated that Jenny is pretty suspicious of other animals. I am unsure if it is because of her past, because of her genetics, or most probably, a combination of both. But once she makes the initial greeting under controlled circumstances, she will get along with most other dogs. But pack behavior is dominant, and that is not unlike our sin behavior when we let it rule in our lives. We don't necessarily want to sin. We merely want to be in control of our behaviors, even if that behavior may be offensive to our Master. But it's our nature. And nature is a powerful force. We may struggle for years to overcome some character deficit, even if we are aware we have it. That doesn't mean we cannot change; it simply means we have to work on it. But with each of our flaws comes a desirable trait as well.

Sometimes anger hides a driven personality. Sometimes shyness covers up a gentle soul. We must make ourselves relax in the joy of revelation as God reveals others to us and learn to not live our lives in a knee-jerk, reactive manner. As we do this, and allow God's Holy Spirit to show us good intent as well as evil, we have an opportunity to be blessed by all those He sends our way. He certainly is able to do that. But we must be paying attention when He does. That applies to any revelation but so much more toward our association with others, for God will reveal both good and evil intent to us if we are paying attention. Jenny is suspicious of all other dogs because she has had much pain at the paws of her own kind. That happens to us as well.

But because we are thinking beings and because we are spiritual beings, we are able to overcome those things that will make our lives always on edge, owning no semblance of peace. That is what resting in Christ does.

Proverbs 1:33

But whoever listens to me will dwell safely, And will be secure, without fear of evil.

If we consider each person we meet as an opportunity—an opportunity to share God's love, an opportunity to share goodness with another, an opportunity to both discover and to teach—we will quickly discover that the Lord will inject a bit of Himself into the mix, into the friendship. But if we ignore his advice as we consider those we invite into our lives, then we may invite some undesirable influences into our sphere.

It takes patience to wait on God to show you something. He will. It always applies to what He desires to show you regarding people, things, and situations. It simply applies to life. When we are patient, we will discover that all our patience will be rewarded. In fact, it may well be said that patience is its own reward. That is simply due to the fact that once you learn to be patient, your stress level will drop like a large rock off a steep cliff. Unless, of course, you are the guy on the bomb squad that dismantles the bombs. I don't think anything will help *your* stress level. But get a dog. That will help.

But we may, by studying the word of peace that God offers again and again throughout His Word—the same sentiment as Proverbs 1:33—come to a place in our lives where life is able to not only be accepted but relished and enjoyed for whatever it is—whether the things happening are light or dark, good or evil.

Jenny prays to go outside but only if her master will come as well (see chapter 3). My greatest desire in life is to go every place I can but only if my Master will be there. If He isn't present, I get afraid and stressed. And when He is, I am relaxed and confident, not only in what I am doing but in what I am saying and thinking as well. We are offered so much from Him that will be with us throughout eternity. These things He offers are worth more than money, cars, houses, and stuff. For they give us the light of only what is shone both by Him and on Him. They give us what is good.

I believe Jenny trusts in this verse:

Psalms 23:4

> *Yea, though I walk through the valley of the shadow of death, I will fear no evil; For You are with me; Your rod and Your staff, they comfort me.*

I trust it too. Because she knows, as I do, that whether it is the staff that guides or the rod that corrects, both are necessary; so both are welcome.

It is quite normal to desire to run with the pack, but speaking as a former pack member, I understand that not all packs are up to doing good, either for themselves or others. It's a choice, though, and it's a choice we must all make.

Jenny has chosen the good, the right, so that she has more easily turned from her dark situation and entered into a place of comfort and love. If she had used her situation in her early years as an excuse to be mean or just plain aggressive, I would not have offered her a home. It was her kindness that drew me in, and it was her gentleness that convinced me that we could develop a friendship that would last.

If each of us could learn that same exact method of turning our defeats, our trials, and our difficulties into joy and kindness and love, we would discover our relationship with the Lord could be one of pure joy, no matter what we have experienced. For our joy would certainly not depend on our situation but we will rather build our relationship—not only with God but with everyone we encounter.

DAVID ROSS SHERMAN

CHAPTER SEVEN

Can You Hear Me Now?

WE ALL SUFFER from lack of attention. We are often curious if God is listening to us. Can He really hear what we are asking and saying to Him? Does He really offer solutions to our situations or those things with which we struggle, or does He just lay out a list of rules to be followed? I guess what I'm saying is, can He hear us? Jenny often suffers from selective hearing, and part of the problem is that she cannot speak. You see, a dialogue requires that two people communicate. But here's my problem regarding this subject: Jenny attempts to solicit information to my understanding but is unable. It's not because she doesn't understand what she says but because I don't. She has a basic understanding of what she is attempting to get across to me, but I don't speak dog. I, though, through sometimes very much effort and training, am able to make her understand what I am attempting to teach her.

From just learning to heel (walking with her head at the same position as my rear right or left heel when I am in full stride), to come, or to lie down, some teaching of her and learning by her is required.

God has the same problem with us.

Here's the big difference though: God is able to understand us . . . completely. He never fails to understand us, but we have a similar problem, just as I do with Jenny and with God. I don't understand her, and I don't understand God, at least not always. I hate it when I can't figure out what He's attempting to tell me, but He is patient and gives me plenty of time. I must be patient with Jenny as well. She really tries hard to understand and to get it, and I know this because I see an improvement or at least a change in frequency of errant behavior, so she is definitely trying.

I hope God sees the same thing in me. God has told me as He tells everyone that to hear is good, but to listen, to heed, and to change our behavior as He instructs us to do is better. I would have much less enjoyment of Jenny if she never changed her behavior, for I would not desire to spend time with a dog that always reacted to things as she did when she first came to live with my wife and me. She barked at everything aggressively. I had to gently teach her that nothing would harm her as long as she was with me. It's a long and arduous process, but once at the goal, she will always be a dog that is a pleasure to accompany.

Could it be that God looks at us exactly the same way?

I mean, when we compare the greatness, the power, the knowledge, and the understanding of God with regard to us, a comparison of my intellect and ability to understand and other things that describe me to Jenny is quite fair. However, I think the differences between humans and God is ten thousand times greater than the differences between the dumbest animals and the most intelligent of humans.

There is a basic problem with seeking God's advice. We often don't know it when we hear His voice. We don't spend enough time listening to Him in order to be able to recognize His voice. Jesus mentioned this in John 10:27:

> *My sheep hear My voice, and I know them, and they follow Me.*

My sheep hear my voice, but the most important part is the second part. They follow me. They follow me . . .they follow me. That is quite a concept. But we cannot do the second part unless we do the first. We must hear His voice. Wow!

So in a *logical* path, we will seek Him, to which He promises that we will find Him. If we find Him, it must follow that He has in some way communicated to us. So at the very first, the very beginning, when we have first come to Him, we have heard Him speak to us. We have felt Him nudge us, and we have, in some way, been in communication with His Holy Spirit. Were it not so we would not be able to be where we are, pledging our love and loyalty to Him. So with that in mind, if you feel that God is not communicating with you or you feel that God has never communicated with you, then you must ask yourself, how did I get to this place?

God speaks to each of us differently, but He speaks to us. There is no one who is truly a Christian who has not heard the voice of God calling them. The call may have come through a human voice, but the urging, the tug on your heart, the voice that says, "Please respond, please answer that question, walk to the front, raise your hand, just take one step toward me," well, that's the voice of God. It is still and small, not loud and threatening. It is gentle and loving, like its owner.

I learned from a teacher so very many years ago that if you want children to hear what you're saying, speak softer, not louder. When God speaks to us, He speaks softly and with great kindness. If and when He speaks to you loudly, there will be no doubt in your mind that it is He who speaks. One of the great problems in hearing Him is that we just tend to talk over Him. We rattle off prayers like they are all He wants to hear rather than to listen to Him and have a conversation, which is always two speaking. We desire that He hears us but forget the part where Jesus said, "My sheep *hear* My voice." He does mention that He knows them.

Only the knowledge of God, which He desires to let us understand, can be understood by mankind. We do not have even a basic understanding of how something is created from nothing.

Go ahead. Try it. If you can do it, I would give you everything I have. So will many others. That's why I say that everything I have belongs to God. He is God and has supplied all I have and all I am, and He will never leave me no matter what happens to me. He protects me continually from some pretty vicious attacks. If you could do that for anyone, then there would be some who would give you everything they have, for they will understand you to be God. Jenny thinks that of me. She gives me everything she has. I like it, she likes it, and it's all good.

That doesn't mean that she always acts as I would like her to act. But she always struggles to improve. And that's pretty good, as far as I'm concerned. I have a modicum more of intelligence than Jenny, though. I should be able to grasp the basics without too much difficulty.

But I don't, at least that's what I show sometimes.

The basics are these:

John 14:6–7

> *Jesus said to him, "I am the way, the truth, and the life. No one comes to the Father except through Me. If you had known Me, you would have known My Father also; and from now on you know Him and have seen Him."*

DAVID ROSS SHERMAN

This alone should give us pause to reflect upon our behavior. To know Jesus is to know the Father, God, and the Creator. Why would anyone presume to enter into His presence unless they are holy? It's dangerous. When we observe Jesus, we have a vision of the Father, God, and the Creator. But we have the ability of the precious gift of grace. We have the gift of the divine influence on our heart and the reflection of that influence in our lives. That is grace.

So if God gives us the ability to act like Him, to be like Him, to love like Him, and to own every bit of joy He owns, do you think it might be a tad bit foolish to ignore that gift? Knowing God is to desire more of Him in your life. It can be no other way. If one fails at that particular thing—the desire for God—then it may be that person does not really own salvation, for the evidence of salvation is that we love God above all other people, places, and things and that we love our neighbor at least as much as we love ourselves.

If we love someone above all other things, we spend time with that person. If we love someone above all other things, when we are not with that person, we are anxious until we can be with Him again.

That is what God wants from us. Jenny never has a problem with that. I work a lot in my woodshop. Jenny doesn't like to be in there too much. It stinks, it's noisy, and it's downright dangerous. She will come in, however reluctantly, for a few minutes when I first go in, but she will leave in a matter of moments. If I start any saws, she exits quickly. She can't do what I can do, but her desire to be with me is strong, and she will come for a while. When she exits, she always stops and looks at me for a moment to see if I might beckon her to stay. If I don't, she will merely walk outside to the sidewalk between the house and the shop and lie down until I come out. When I do come out, she jumps up, tail wagging, to show her pleasure at being reunited with me. I am sure to always give her a little love and some comforting words for waiting patiently.

God wants us to wait for Him as well. When we do, we are always better off because of it. The most amazing life can be ours if we learn to really listen for His voice and then wait for Him to direct us before we move in any direction. Jenny taught me that she knows she is safer while she is near me. I only hope I can learn that lesson when it comes to being near to God.

CHAPTER EIGHT

I Will Find You, and You Will Give Me Love

A SEDENTARY LIFESTYLE is a fairly common thing for most dogs, unless they are mushing in the Klondike or working as a search-and-rescue dog or any such similar thing. Jenny has never been harnessed to a sled. She may enjoy searching for a bone and rescuing it from my hand, but for the most part, she lies around and waits to work until the last moment possible.

That is, once again, unless it is outside. I have already said how she loves the outdoors, but she loves the ritual we employ nearly every day—hide-and-seek on the driveway and front yard. Here's how it works: I go out on the driveway and make a sudden, jerky motion like I'm about to take off, and she begins to run. She will run back and forth past me four or five times, and then she will run to each side of the circular driveway and mark it. I will act like I'm going back inside, and she will bolt past me. It is then I take off in the other direction and hide. When she realizes I am not there, she will come looking. Of course, she always finds me. She knows my scent, and she follows it. But it makes me feel good to know that she doesn't just wait for me to come back. She chases me until she finds me. She pursues me with all her energy.

Just as Jenny won't allow me to separate myself from her, we should be exactly the same way with God. He desires that we pursue Him, and He has promised us that if we just seek Him, we will find Him.

Deuteronomy 4:29

> *But from there you will seek the Lord your God, and you will find Him if you seek Him with all your heart and with all your soul.*

And there is the key: seek Him with all your heart and soul. That is the problem we face in so many ways and during our limited time during each day. But that's the only way we will discover God, and it is due to that little two-lettered word there, *if*. But I will let you in on a little secret. It is not difficult. It is never as much work as it may seem at the outset, even though it does require all your heart and all your soul.

Jenny never minds searching for me for she knows she will find me. She focuses on the reward. She prepares her heart in the moment it takes to realize I am not with her, and she chases me with great enthusiasm. Her autonomic responses take over, and those are her soul. But it is her heart, her desire to find me, that makes her go, makes her face any obstacle, for she knows she will find the prize—me—and I will give her love, which is all the reward she seeks.

Wouldn't it be awesome to think of our pursuit of God that way? Wouldn't it be so wonderful to know that the end of our pursuit, the end of our journey, would be the reward of being with our Master? With that mind-set, we will never stop seeking Him, with all our heart and with great enthusiasm. Jenny has figured that it's more fun if she is enthusiastic about it. We can all learn that lesson. When we begin to lose our enthusiasm, we will discover that other things will soon creep into our minds, and then our bodies will soon follow. But the cost of being a disciple of Jesus is great. It doesn't cost us 10 percent of what we earn or any other material thing. It costs us everything.

The cost of being a disciple of Jesus is everything. You see, there's a word that we must become intimately familiar with if we are to truly understand what it means to be a disciple. It's the word *repent*. The word *repent* in Greek is an interesting word. It is the word *metanoeo* (repent) when used as a verb and the word *metanoia* (repentance) when it's a noun. But either way, it means two things are happening at once. First of all, it's the compunction or sadness at having done a particular act. Once you get to know God pretty well, you will feel that compunction at just having offended Him, but even if you don't know Him well, you will more than likely feel bad. The second thing it means is to think again, or think differently, after having experienced such sadness. It means to change your mind, your direction, your intention, your heart.

Here's the problem: we think that it will never happen again. We somehow are able to convince ourselves that it is done. We really want to go and sin no more, but we have to face that torture, that unbearable desire, and that horrible temptation. So we falter and fall again and again while seemingly unable to conquer, to overcome, to win the victory.

But that is exactly why we must begin to seek. Seeking involves chasing the knowledge of God, and the knowledge of God is what allows us to discover all we need to know to understand how to have a complete and full life—both here and eternally. The goal is to discover in our lives, in every single aspect of our lives, the fruit of the Spirit. We find the nine things we refer to as the fruit of the Spirit in Paul's letter to the church in Galatia. They are love, joy, peace, long-suffering (patience), kindness, goodness, faithfulness, gentleness, and self-control (Galatians 5:22–23).

So when you are stirred to minister to someone, do you have love in that ministry? Do you have joy in that ministry? Peace? Patience? You get the picture. But even when you are in a conversation with someone, are love and peace and gentleness and the other things in this list present in that conversation?

When you are at work, when you are driving, and when you are in prayer, the goal of every Christian should be these nine things. But without seeking them, you will not find them. Without researching when Jesus exhibited these things, or Paul or Elijah or Joseph or Abraham, we will never discover when we should attempt to display one of these things in our own life. Jesus is always the template for the Christian believer, but we should also look at others who were used by God to give His people hope and a purpose. Perhaps we can do the same for someone.

I cannot emphasize enough how important it is to keep seeking God, no matter how much knowledge you may have of God, no matter how long you have known Him, and no matter what experience you may have had either with Him or with others regarding God. For we cannot know the depth of God; we cannot know the depth of the love of God. Paul says it this way in Ephesians 3:17–19:

> *That Christ may dwell in your hearts through faith; that you, being rooted and grounded in love, may be able to comprehend with all the saints what is the width and length and depth and height—to know the love of Christ*

which passes knowledge; that you may be filled with all the fullness of God.

Although we may never understand fully the love of Christ, for it is beyond that which may be understood by man, if Christ dwells in our hearts, through our faith, we will be or we will become rooted and grounded in love; and with love—because of love—we will begin (just begin, mind you) to comprehend the magnificent love of God for His creation, us. And because of the gifts He gives us, all of us—whether those gifts be physical or spiritual or mental or emotional gifts, whether they be small or great, whether they be singular or even if you are blessed with many—there is but one way to utilize that gift or gifts that will have eternal implications, and that is to utilize your talent, your gift, your ability for the glory of God.

And to do that, you must seek humility for to use your gifts and abilities in this manner is to take the low road and to never mention how you did something for another person. For if you were truly doing it for the Lord, to glorify Him, then you would have realized that it wasn't you; it was Jesus in you. You must seek to *metanoeo*. You must seek to think differently.

You may use your talent and all your abilities for worldly purposes, and you may become quite successful in the world. But that will do nothing for you beyond this life. Eternity is a place of habitation, and so it is a dwelling forever. Of much greater importance in this life is what is done for Christ and in the name of Christ. And according to Paul, nothing, absolutely nothing, is as important in this life as what can be learned of God. He said in Philippians 3:8,

> *Yet indeed I also count all things loss for the excellence of the knowledge of Christ Jesus my Lord, for whom I have suffered the loss of all things, and count them as rubbish, that I may gain Christ.*

Just a few verses later, Paul states that he hasn't grasped it all yet that is to say, he isn't done learning. So he isn't done seeking yet, but he is keeping his eyes on Jesus. He said in Philippians 3:12–14,

DAVID ROSS SHERMAN

Not that I have already attained, or am already perfected; but I press on, that I may lay hold of that for which Christ Jesus has also laid hold of me. Brethren, I do not count myself to have apprehended; but one thing I do, forgetting those things which are behind and reaching forward to those things which are ahead, I press toward the goal for the prize of the upward call of God in Christ Jesus.

In his seeking, he is moving ever toward the goal of Christ, moving always toward Jesus, being more like Him every day, overcoming those things of the world, and discovering more of God in him each day. He is becoming a transformed being—one who searches for God in anything and finds Him in everything.

When we can uncover God in us, in all that we do and say and think, we are certainly moving in the right direction. But never should we think we are finished, for the knowledge of God is unending and the ways we are able to improve our being, whether through actions or words or even thoughts, are so numerous that I am unable to even put them into words.

Let me just say that we can all use a little more God and a little less world and flesh in our lives. We need not be stuffy and without smiles and laughter for our God is a god of joy. Remember that joy is the second thing after love on that list of nine fruits of the Spirit. We should be a joyous bunch of people. And for many reasons. I hope I don't have to point them out to you. Just look around, you'll see enough to make your heart fill with joy. This is an amazing place, and we are an even more amazing creation that God has chosen to bless with so many possibilities. And though it is true that we are the top of the line when it comes to God's creations, it is also true that we are not complete unless we are filled with His Spirit.

We can be a lot. We can own billions of dollars in real estate and stocks. We can live in mansions of gold or have many servants and big cars, but without God in our lives, we are indeed very poor and wretched.

The church in Laodicea had no idea that they fit that bill. Laodicea was a very rich place, which had very wealthy citizens, but Jesus called them out in His address to the churches in the Revelation 3:15–17:

I know your works, that you are neither cold nor hot. I could wish you were cold or hot. So then, because you are lukewarm, and neither cold nor hot, I will vomit you out of My mouth. Because you say, "I am rich, have become wealthy, and have need of nothing"—and do not know that you are wretched, miserable, poor, blind, and naked.

These folks had no idea how much danger they were in, and Jesus was attempting to warn them. But He didn't leave them without help or direction for He said this in Revelation 3:18–20:

I counsel you to buy from Me gold refined in the fire, that you may be rich; and white garments, that you may be clothed, that the shame of your nakedness may not be revealed; and anoint your eyes with eye salve, that you may see. As many as I love, I rebuke and chasten. Therefore be zealous and repent.

Please understand that those living in Laodicea, or anywhere else for that matter, are able to return. But they must think again. They must change the way they think of their sin—that dark part of them that desires to satisfy the flesh and receive the world. They must reconsider who they are in Christ and make a decision to stand with Him for He is knocking.

Revelation 3:20

Behold, I stand at the door and knock. If anyone hears My voice and opens the door, I will come in to him and dine with him, and he with Me.

Jesus was willing to receive those living in Laodicea, and He is willing to receive all those who come to Him. And this one thing will happen when we turn to Christ fully in our lives.

Revelation 3:21–22

To him who overcomes I will grant to sit with Me on My throne, as I also overcame and sat down with My Father on His throne. He who has an ear, let him hear what the Spirit says to the churches.

Seeking God with all our heart will enable us to overcome the world, our own flesh, and the enemy of God. Because as we seek Him with all our heart, we will discover that He lives within us and will assist us as we overcome those things that challenge, those things that threaten to remove us from His presence, and those things in our lives that put us in that place of darkness, sadness, and misery.

If, like Jenny, we are able to chase with reckless abandon our Master, never losing His scent and imagining what joy and gladness will fill our hearts when we once again reconnect, then our mind will never again concern itself with anything else, whether it is painful or satisfying to our senses, for our senses will be filled with only God. We will find Him, and He will give us love.

CHAPTER NINE

Oh, Now I Get It!

DOGS LEARN, LIKE people, at varying paces and in different ways. Jenny takes a moment or two to understand, and by that, I mean an hour or a day or a week or two or possibly a lifetime of constant reminding of what I am attempting to teach her. But it must be exactly as I want it, or it isn't really training. I expect her to do just what I want for she must learn two things from this aspect of training, obedience and trust. Trust that I am teaching her this for her own good and for my service. Sometimes it is for her own safety. For example, I am in the process of teaching her to never respond to any passing sound, passing vehicle, or passing animal. This is a very long process, for it is in her very nature to react to just these things. To teach her this, I must maintain a quiet demeanor myself. I must never react to those things to which I am asking her to not react. Cesar Milan calls it our energy, and that is exactly what it is. Dogs read people very well. Jenny reacts to negative energy in a negative way. She must learn to not react to it at all in order to be acceptable in many social situations.

But she is learning. Slowly and thoroughly, she is learning. And that is the key—thorough. Never return to the old ways. That's when training is done. An adulteress was brought to Jesus for some judgment, and He instead gave those who brought her training. He was asked what should be done to her.

John 8:3–11

> *When the scribes and Pharisees brought to Him a woman caught in adultery. And when they had set her in the midst, they said to Him, "Teacher, this woman was caught in adultery, in the very act. Now Moses, in the*

law, commanded us that such should be stoned. But what do You say?"

This they said, testing Him, that they might have something of which to accuse Him. But Jesus stooped down and wrote on the ground with His finger, as though He did not hear. So when they continued asking Him, He raised Himself up and said to them, "He who is without sin among you, let him throw a stone at her first."

And again He stooped down and wrote on the ground.

Then those who heard it, being convicted by their conscience, went out one by one, beginning with the oldest even to the last. And Jesus was left alone, and the woman standing in the midst. When Jesus had raised Himself up and saw no one but the woman, He said to her, "Woman, where are those accusers of yours? Has no one condemned you?" She said, "No one, Lord." And Jesus said to her, "Neither do I condemn you; go and sin no more."

Jesus was offering two things, forgiveness and opportunity. He removed the death sentence from her by simply saying He didn't condemn her. But now she must look at her circumstances, look at her behavior, and change so she is able to line up with the One who saved her from certain death. For if He was able to do it this time, perhaps it is an eternal thing.

Jenny understands that I am sometimes not happy with her behavior. I want her to change. I want her to learn to never give her position away by barking at something that poses no danger. I want her to learn to never react to another animal just because it is there. I want her to stop eating the cat's food. These are things she needs to change. But they are part of her basic makeup, and so they are difficult to learn. Change is just plain hard. Change requires an inward transition, which is an extremely difficult thing. As I explained before, it is a new thinking that is required. She must learn to learn. So must we.

Without both the inward change and the outward evidence, there is really no change at all. For us, without the specific change of heart that

DAVID ROSS SHERMAN

can *only* happen through the work of the Holy Spirit, any change that occurs is merely us attempting to go and sin no more or go and do some good works or go and do something, anything, under our own power.

It is not that our attempting change without God is a bad thing, but it is most certainly an incomplete thing, and much more often than not, it is something that will not last. But we must clear up any misconceptions that we may hold regarding the Holy Spirit, His work in our lives, and our part in the change that happens to us as He begins and continues to work within us.

There are things that must come together in us in order to help us affect change in our lives. In fact, every single good thing we have ever learned—those things that strengthen, those things that encourage, and those things that empower us to move out of ourselves and into a life in Christ—are all useful in accomplishing change in our lives. And we can never say, "Well, that was a waste of time. It really didn't help me at all to say no that one time because the next week, there I was, doing the same old thing."

What we might miss is that each time we overcome, we are blessed and have drawn closer to God. I know that no one is changed immediately, and most return to their sin or sins after they begin a relationship with the Lord. That is why there is a need for churches—for studying the Word or for having a relationship with God—for once begun, if we were made perfect, there would be no need for further study or relationship. How many who are reading this are perfect? I will give you your money back for the book. But the people who know you best must be the judge.

Even the word *relationship* in itself implies an area of growth between two. And it requires time to build wherein we grow in the knowledge of one another and discover those things that make us want to know even better the one we have chosen to be with, whom we can relate to. When we have a relationship with God, we might surmise that we are never going to be able to know totally the One who has spoken the universe into existence, who has created everything that has ever existed, and who is, without a doubt, the most complex being who has ever been.

Jenny has a great deal of desire to please her master, but the draw of what she is both genetically and through breeding while factoring in her history, and I am left with a friend who struggles often with her desire to be herself and the desire to please me. Our relationship is not based on her behavior, though. I love her and care for her no matter what she does, and she is secure in that relationship. But each time she overcomes her desire and pleases me by not reacting to some stimulus or not eating the cat's food, she is rewarded by an acknowledgement of her good behavior. She gets it. After many times of that scenario repeating itself, she has a new behavior.

We don't even understand ourselves to any degree of success. Otherwise we would never suffer from depression, never get angry, and never sin. Our desire to be fulfilled is what drives us to sin, and our lack of fulfillment is what causes us to be depressed and angry and to feel every other human emotion. We must be filled. We *will* be filled with something. We have an offer from God to be filled with Him, and yet we just don't seem to be able to understand why that is a good thing. Jesus promised this filling in John 14:15–17:

> *If you love Me, keep My commandments. And I will pray the Father, and He will give you another Helper, that He may abide with you forever—the Spirit of truth, whom the world cannot receive, because it neither sees Him nor knows Him; but you know Him, for He dwells with you and will be in you.*

Some manuscripts read, "If you love me, you will keep my commandments." And that is probably more accurate. If we love Him, the evidence will be that we keep His commandments. You see, we can't live in both worlds at the same time. Knowing Him or loving Him is meant to affect a change in our lives and assist us in our battles to overcome the enemy of our soul.

I have met so many in my life who, whenever they are living at peace with God, living in a holy manner, keeping themselves from sin, and studying the Word, are, without a doubt, the happiest people I have ever known. Yet it rarely lasts. They run back, sometimes for a moment and sometimes for very long periods, to enjoy those things they left behind when they came to the Lord. And to be quite honest, I have done exactly the same thing.

And while they are there, they absolutely hate themselves. They are miserable. Peter calls it a dog returning to its own vomit (2 Peter 2:22). Not a very pretty picture, but one that each of us understands.

As the Spirit of God fills us up, we will grow less and less inclined to bring darkness into our soul because His light is filling us. At least that's the way it's supposed to work. The thing we must remember is that we will always have free will, which will be there to give us the ability in a matter of seconds to turn the switch off to that light. Some of us flip it on and off like a strobe light. So we must continually ask Him to be present in us, to make us aware of His presence, and to bring us to our knees when we find ourselves headed toward the light switch.

In the sixth chapter of Paul's first letter to the Corinthians, he makes some very disturbing comments. At least they are disturbing to anyone who may be caught up in some sort of sin. In 1 Corinthians 6:9, he asks a question that is really resounding to those who may think they can live in two worlds at once.

> *Do you not know that the unrighteous will not inherit the kingdom of God?*

But after that, he makes a relatively scary statement, "Do not be deceived." For many years, there was a teaching that circulated in the church. We were told it wasn't possible to be deceived if we were Christians because Christians are filled with the Holy Spirit. Obviously, that isn't true. I would say that it is more likely that we choose to be deceived or we welcome deception because we look at it as a way to return to that vomit. And we justify it by saying we were just deceived. But then Paul gives us a laundry list of sins.

1 Corinthians 6:9–10

> *Do you not know that the unrighteous will not inherit the kingdom of God? Do not be deceived. Neither fornicators, nor idolaters, nor adulterers, nor homosexuals, nor sodomites, nor thieves, nor covetous, nor drunkards, nor revilers, nor extortioners will inherit the kingdom of God.*

Now that's quite a list, and it seems fairly comprehensive. But when you look at these things individually, they can include a lot of other things that, at first, you may not consider part of the list. Idolaters are like that. They can make idols out of almost anything or anyone.

In verse 17 of this chapter, Paul tells us that when we are joined to the Lord and when we make that move to ask Him to allow us to be His children, to forgive us, and to come into us, we become one with Him. That's a pretty amazing thing, don't you think? To be one with the living God is truly one of the most incredible things that could possibly happen to us as humans.

Although Jenny is an amazing animal and has a wonderful connection with me, she can never be *one* with me. She is certainly able to please me, to warn me, and to defend me (even when I don't need defending), but she just can't be one with me. Being one with someone means that you know how they think, how they will react to a situation, and how they are. When we become one with the Father, we become a place of residence for God. We become a temple. We are the temple of God; it is the place He resides. He allows his Holy Spirit to dwell within us, and as if that were not enough, Paul adds another statement that is meant to make us grasp the severity of the situation: *and you are not your own.*

When we sin, when we walk into unrighteousness, we do not only darken our souls but we also attempt to darken the Holy Spirit. Is it any wonder why God is saddened by our sin? Our flesh is constantly attempting to be fulfilled by food, money, sex, power, and a thousand other things that will never satisfy our spirits. For there is but One who can satisfy anything other than our flesh, and that is God.

We have to look back a bit in this same letter to fully grasp what Paul is attempting to tell us through this letter to the church in Corinth. You see, I believe that God is able to work with each one of us to help us understand exactly what it is we need to understand in order to grasp these truths. God doesn't desire for us to be left stranded and lost without hope. And He certainly doesn't desire that we be beaten over the head with threats in order to be true followers of Christ. He desires that we become new creatures simply because He knows we will self-destruct if we face Him in unrighteousness.

If we look at the second chapter of this first letter to the Corinthians, you will see what I mean.

1 Corinthians 2:9–11

But as it is written: "Eye has not seen, nor ear heard, Nor have entered into the heart of man The things which God has prepared for those who love Him." But God has revealed them to us through His Spirit. For the Spirit searches all things, yes, the deep things of God. For what man knows the things of a man except the spirit of the man which is in him? Even so no one knows the things of God except the Spirit of God.

Jenny cannot understand why I desire her to act in a particular way or do a particular thing. She does understand that some things really please her master. She cannot understand that I am preparing her for possible future events. We cannot understand why and what God has made us ready for—as far as knowledge, as far as understanding, as far as preparation for the events of the future, and as far as anything in our lives that has happened, is happening, or will happen—because we could not have any understanding of events that are in front of us. I look back on some events in my life and wondered why they happened, but as the years passed by, the light went on.

I have a friend who called me a while back and told me he just got out of jail. He is not the kind of guy who would be arrested for anything. It seems that he had an old traffic ticket, but after the ticket was issued, he moved, and they sent it to his old address. A warrant was issued. They stopped him for some infraction, saw that there was a warrant, and took him to jail in a nearby town. He began reciting scriptures in his cell and praying. Before the night was over, he led four people in the jail to the Lord. God knew about this more than a couple of thousand years ago. God put all the things in motion for this to happen. My friend was released the next day. Paul continues in verses 12–13,

Now we have received, not the spirit of the world, but the Spirit who is from God, that we might know the things that have been freely given to us by God. These things we also speak, not in words which man's wisdom teaches but which the Holy Spirit teaches, comparing spiritual things with spiritual.

I work patiently with Jenny to teach her how I want her to be. But I have learned that I must be a gentle teacher for she is bruised; she has been mistreated and needs to learn to trust me. I cannot force her to do what I desire, so patience is the key. The Holy Spirit is within us to teach us, to prepare us, to lead us, and to convict us. But in all this, He will not force us to do what we should. God desires to use us in many ways, in many places, at many times. But two things prevent us from being used: we have sin in our lives, or we are not making ourselves available. And what I mean by available is the fact that we surrender our availability.

Do you realize how many things we miss simply because we do not make ourselves available? Let us just say a lot. And much of the time, we are not available because we are satisfying our flesh rather than our spirit. In those cases, the devil gets a twofer. And we were part of his plan. When we refuse to surrender our anger to anything, we hurt the one to whom we show anger, and we miss the opportunity to show love, even if that person is unloving to us or does something without proper thought.

When we place anything or anyone before God in our lives by not surrendering those things or persons and putting them behind God, not only do we make them an idol but we also miss the opportunity to satisfy our spirit by exposing ourselves to God's Word, God's praise, and God's wonder. And all the time, we could have shared God's Word, God's praise, and God's wonder with the very one we have placed in front of Him.

I am always pleased when Jenny finally gets it and when she finally understands what it is I am asking her to do. We both rejoice—her in the learning and I in the teaching. And it is a great day in our house. And when we finally get it, when we finally understand how we should be and how we may please our Master, it is indeed a great day in the kingdom.

Knowing God, committing ourselves to God (and keeping that commitment), living in the grace of God, and living always within the confines of the joy of God, we will discover that the Holy Spirit will do what He does and give us all we can have of God. When we surrender all we have—our will, our very lives—and give it all to Him, we will surely discover that His imagination will spill over into all we think, say, and do. Then and only then, the mind we own will be the mind

DAVID ROSS SHERMAN

of Christ, the voice we use will be the voice of God, and the feet with which we walk and the hands we use to act will be under the control of the Holy Spirit.

CHAPTER TEN

Don't Worry; I'll Protect You

F EAR IS AN ugly thing. It can ruin your day and usually for no reason, for most of the fear we have in our lives is unfounded. Many of us can look back on times when we were fearful and laugh at how what we thought was the end or very near that turned out to be a great learning experience. But it left us a bit more wary of things that come at us.

Then there are the triggers—the things that make us remember the times we were in fear—and for good reason. Our world may have been falling apart, our lives filled with despair and grief, and although we may have survived, we are scarred. We are forever forced to have, in that hallowed place that should be occupied by thoughts of bright colors and laughter and smiling faces, memories of darkness and evil instead, whose desire it is to bring us back as often as possible.

Jenny has lived in that place of fear, and she can return instantly to that place of fear, even though there is nothing to fear. But because it happened so early in her life, it is indelibly marked in her psyche in a way that presents itself in ways that sometimes break my heart. She hates loud noises. I don't know why, but she absolutely hates anything loud. Actually, I do know why. She can hear a car from half a mile away and another dog bark from farther than that. So that is part of it. But if a voice is raised even a little bit, she will display a nervousness that betrays her troubled heart. I am unsure of what happened to create this condition, but it is indeed sad to see the fear that grips her when someone gets loud. If it is I who has gotten loud, however, she will come to my side and attempt to comfort me in a way that offers both support and understanding. She will place her head next to my leg, pushing ever so gently until she feels me return to a calmness she enjoys. I am never sure if it's for my benefit or hers, but whichever one—it works.

Thunder is another nail-biter for Jenny. She has exhibited some fairly complicated gymnastics and secured some unusual hiding places when thunder is happening. I found her in the shower one night during a bad thunderstorm, shivering with fear. I put her bed in there, but when I left, she did as well. No surprise. She has gotten better, but I am unsure if the terror of the storm will ever depart from her.

Jenny knows that I will comfort her fears no matter what those fears may entail. I don't mock her or laugh at her, even though what I may be witnessing may be laughable. I never think it's funny to see an animal or human in a terrified state. So if she needs comfort, I will get on the floor with her and wrap my arms around her and just hold her. It's what my Father does for me, so I just pass it along. But it's also what Jenny does for me when I am in need of something I can't explain. She just understands. I have seen her overcome her own fears to try to comfort me, and that is a true friend because fear is such a powerful thing that it can overcome much of what we come to expect from one another.

Fear can even overcome our faith in so very many situations. We, as humans, can have so many fears—fear of being alone, of death, of rejection, of being misunderstood, of pain, of not having financial security, of failure, of the unknown, of not knowing God's will or even knowing God's will, of man or, even scarier to men . . . woman. And the scariest thing of all to so many of both genders . . . relationships.

Some people have one of these fears. Some have many. To have even one is difficult, but to have a bunch of these and to live within the confines of these kinds of prisons is, to say the least, horrible. I can guarantee that God does not want us to live like that.

So how do we overcome fear? Perhaps it will be easier to discuss how we manage to invite fear into our lives. Now please understand that fear is not altogether a bad thing. God built it into our very being so that we would become cautious. If you're out walking in a dangerous place, it's a good thing to be cautious. And these days, much of the world is a dangerous place. A little fear will contribute to that caution. Be safe. But if your fear makes you curl up in a ball and lie on the ground, then your fear has overcome you.

When Paul wrote to Timothy in 2 Timothy 1:6–8, he said,

> *Therefore I remind you to stir up the gift of God which is in you through the laying on of my hands. For God has not*

given us a spirit of fear, but of power and of love and of a sound mind. Therefore do not be ashamed of the testimony of our Lord, nor of me His prisoner, but share with me in the sufferings for the gospel according to the power of God.

He spoke of fear here, but in the context in which he was speaking and the word he used that is interpreted as *fear*, it has more to do with not being timid in preaching the Gospel of Jesus, even if he may be made to suffer for that same Gospel. But this was likely only a few weeks before Paul was beheaded, so it is quite possible that Paul was attempting to still the fears his young protégé was experiencing.

We all have fear. And the list I showed you a few paragraphs ago is a short list. There are so many things in this world that may spawn fear, but it is up to us to discover the truth of who is in control. And that is the key. This key has a few different notches in it that all work together to open the lock that is held together by fear.

The first is truth. Truth is not whatever you think it might be; it is not what you think it is. Truth is what it is. Jesus was quite clear and spoke with not the slightest trace of ambiguity when He said, "I am the way, the truth, and the life." He is *the* truth, and there can only be one truth. We must never lose sight of that.

The second notch is faith. It's that two-edged sword of which I speak so often. Not merely believing in that which is not seen but making that which is unseen believable by your actions and deeds. When people can see Jesus in you, they can see Jesus. When you know the truth, your faith is made clear in your life.

And the last notch is trust. We must learn to trust the One who has brought us the truth. And if you truly have faith, if you really own faith in that truth, then your trust will be wholeheartedly in Him. It is really easy to speak this, but to know that the truth is in your heart can only come to light by how that truth is revealed in you. It could be that if you have fear operating in your life, then you really don't trust in God. Your faith is not where it needs to be because the truth you understand is not the truth that Christ has revealed.

Fear is a tool of the devil. It is used by him to keep you from operating at the fullness in which God desires you to operate. It is meant to keep you from being filled with the Holy Spirit and developing fully

DAVID ROSS SHERMAN

your relationship with God. It used by the enemy to make you believe a lie.

And those lies can be the following:

- You are so lonely.
- You'll die a horrible death.
- You're going to be rejected.
- No one will ever understand you.
- You're going to have so much pain in your life.
- There will never be any financial security for you.
- You're a failure.
- There is no truth; everything is unknown.
- Everyone wants to hurt you, so you will never have any positive relationships in your life.

If you believe these things as truths, it sucks being you. And you have no faith that God is able to accomplish His truth in your life. The only way to get out of that situation is to study His truth and see how it has been working in your life. Perhaps that is what Roosevelt meant by, "The only thing to fear is fear itself." None of these things are real. The truth is what is real, and that truth is found in only one place.

The cure for fear, and I mean all types of fear, is the same. It is to have a deeper trust in God and a growing confidence that He will care for us and help us through any challenges we may need to overcome. And that can only be accomplished by a deep and intimate relationship, and that means we must be involved with the relationship on more than a weekly or even daily basis. To have an intimate relationship, we must be involved all the time—not only during times when we are afraid, not only during times when we are hurting, and not only during times when we don't know what to do next.

Our relationship with God must be when we wake up and when we have that first cup of coffee and when we are going to work and when we are doing the most enjoyable things we can do. He wants to share with us those times as well as the times of difficulty and suffering and pain and fear. He wants to be involved in our lives in a way that will give us the fullness of who He is, in a way that will give us the fullness of who we can become, and it can only happen when we lose our fear due to our relationship with Him.

If Jenny was only near me when I was hurting, or if she only came to me when she was hurting in some way, then the relationship we have would not be one built on trust and a desire to share with one another. Now don't get me wrong. I don't get into deep spiritual conversations with my dog, but she is always ready to acknowledge me and assuage my fears if I become emotional or if some event has stirred me in some way. And I stand ready to give her the same comfort should she need it, but we both know the other is there when the need shows itself.

What we all must realize is that some fears are founded and some are not. Sometimes we have good reason for our fears, and other times, the reason for a particular fear is just invented in our minds. It exists only because we don't know the answer to a particular problem. Fear has come to land on our doorstep simply because our imagination has taken us to the worst-case scenario . . . again.

Of course, bad things *can* happen. Does that mean they *will* happen? Not really. Unless you make them happen. I see people every day that shoot themselves in the foot when it comes to their own lives simply because of their unfounded fears.

For example, I met a young man who was homeless. When I asked him why he was homeless, he merely replied, "I can't find a job." When I asked him how many applications he had put in since he had been in town for two months, he replied, "A couple." When I asked him why he had only put in one or two applications, he said, "Because I was afraid no one would hire me." I asked him why he thought no one would hire him, and he said, "Because I don't have any nice clothes."

I wanted to tell him that there were probably some other reasons as well, but I didn't. We gave him some clothes and a place to stay. We got him cleaned up, and eventually, he was able to get a job and pay his own way. But there was no telling how long that young man would have gone on living in his fears, which I found out were many, had he been allowed to just live in those fears and let them control his life instead of becoming proactive and taking charge.

I believe a little fear is a good thing. It keeps you sharp. It makes you attentive. But a lot of fear—fear that is real and fear that is imagined—will put you in a place you don't desire to be. It's called prison. And you become not just a prisoner of whatever it is you're afraid of but a prisoner of fear itself.

DAVID ROSS SHERMAN

Our enemy uses fear all the time to prevent us from doing something that might shine a little light. Sometimes it is just stupid little fears that aren't really even fears at all. Some of you probably had fears about buying this book. *I don't know if I want to read this book. What's it about? I'm afraid he's going to be talking about stuff I don't want to read. I already know about Jesus . . . I wonder if it's just about Jesus . . .* Since you are reading this, I will assume you overcame your fears. Thank you. I will tell Jenny.

There are a thousand ways that our fears keep us from the Lord. God never intended for that to happen. God instilled fear into us as a protective device—a defense mechanism to make us wary of our enemies and to help protect us when we were in danger—but it was never meant to make us cower in our tracks or grovel before our enemies.

Do you think David had any fear when he walked out to face Goliath? I'm sure he had some fear. However, I don't think his knees were knocking or that he was trembling. I believe that his fear was turned into righteous indignation because this "uncircumcised Philistine" was mocking the God of David. And David knew that he was not alone on that battlefield but that God had put him there to show God's power, not David's. That was why he did not need to fear. He knew that it was not him who was going to take this guy down.

1 Samuel 17:32–37

> *Then David said to Saul, "Let no man's heart fail because of him; your servant will go and fight with this Philistine." And Saul said to David, "You are not able to go against this Philistine to fight with him; for you are a youth, and he a man of war from his youth." But David said to Saul, "Your servant used to keep his father's sheep, and when a lion or a bear came and took a lamb out of the flock, I went out after it and struck it, and delivered the lamb from its mouth; and when it arose against me, I caught it by its beard, and struck and killed it. "Your servant has killed both lion and bear; and this uncircumcised Philistine will be like one of them, seeing he has defied the armies of the living God."*

Moreover David said, "The LORD, who delivered me from the paw of the lion and from the paw of the bear, He will deliver me from the hand of this Philistine." And Saul said to David, "Go, and the LORD be with you!"

Of all the men in the armies of Israel, not one would face this giant who mocked them. It took a shepherd boy who really understood the power of God to show the power of God. One thing that we must understand about David is that he didn't fly into an angry rage, but rather, he had a righteous indignation. Was he upset? Yes. Did he go running on to the field of battle unprepared? Not at all. He prepared.

Now Saul tried to prepare David in Saul's way, the only way he knew, but that didn't work. So David just picked up a few stones, his staff, and his sling and walked out to face this giant called Goliath. Now Goliath was insulted that this young boy had been sent out to fight him, and rightfully so. "Send me a warrior, not a shepherd boy," he cursed David. Now to the untrained ear, it sounded like some trash-talking was going on, but David was just responding with what he knew to be true.

We know the rest of the story and that David wasn't talking trash at all. He was just spouting some prophecy. We all have some Goliaths in our lives or at some point in our lives. And quite often, we want to crumble and just fall apart at the thought of facing that giant. But that isn't where God wants us to be. That is when God desires that we seek Him.

Jenny's fears are lessened by my presence. I am always comforted by her presence, but even more than that, I am comforted by the presence of God. When He reminds me that He is near, I am often overwhelmed by Him just being there, but I always know I can trust Him to protect me and to stand nearby to comfort me as I go through any difficult circumstance. And I know He will always protect me. Jenny knows I will always protect her, and it is good. This is how it's supposed to be.

DAVID ROSS SHERMAN

CHAPTER ELEVEN

I Hate Cats, but You Guys Are OK

O VER MY LIFETIME, I have had quite a few pets. I'm a dog guy but have had many cats too. I love it when different species interact and I am able to witness that interaction.

A few years before Jenny moved in, one of our neighbors moved away and left two cats. One of the reasons I like cats is because they are so very resilient. They know what must be done in order to survive, and they will do it. One of the new kitties I named Fuzzball because she had a lot of fur. But she was a tiny little creature, so skinny and frail. But you would have to pick her up to know that for her fur makes her look like a pretty buff little animal. The other I named Buckwheat for the kid by the same name from the old movie series the *Little Rascals*. She was all black and really had a handle on the neighborhood. She ruled. And she protected Fuzzball because she needed to. In the interest of full disclosure, Buckwheat was really Buckwheat III. I just don't give a lot of thought to cats' names simply because they won't learn them anyway, so why put a lot of effort into it?

We began to feed them as soon as we realized they had been abandoned. They were happy being outdoor cats, even in the winter, and although I did invite them inside at various times, the only one who took me up on the invitation was Buckwheat. That lasted only a day, though. In anticipation of the event, we went out and purchased a litter box, litter, and a bunch of cat-related stuff. Buckwheat could not figure out how to use a litter box. She would relieve herself on the floor right next to it, so she was quickly returned to her place outside.

The day I brought Jenny home with me was her first opportunity to meet both Buckwheat and Fuzzball. Now please understand that all things animal must be worked out by animal means. Sometimes that means allowing personalities and instincts and behaviors to all mesh together and living with the consequences.

When I pulled up into the driveway, I warned Jenny, "You really don't want to wear a cat on your face. Treat them with respect, and they will simply ignore you." I had dogs before that loved to chase cats, at least until they caught one. Cats are not usually aggressive toward other animals but will protect their territory with great fervor. Buckwheat looked at the beast exiting the vehicle and did not budge an inch from her perch on the floor of the landing atop a five-step rise from the ground. We had to walk right in front of her to go in through the front door. Jenny was busy sniffing around the ground to drink in all the new scents, and I could tell by her body language that she was picking up a scent—yes, the scent of kittie! And then she saw it. She bolted up the steps to chase this cat off her new home and got the surprise of a lifetime.

Buckwheat never even stood for the occasion. As Jenny got close enough, Buckwheat just rose up enough to pick up her two front paws and, with claws fully extended, gave Jenny a right-left-right combination that occurred in the blink of an eye. And then Buckwheat rose and walked slowly through the gate. Not in retreat but as if to say, "You just got schooled, doggie. Don't ever mess with me again." Jenny froze at this prospect, and I could tell she didn't understand what had happened. But she calmed herself very quickly. It was a lot to take in for her—new master, new home, new smells, new sounds . . . and not one but two cats. What is happening?

The next time Jenny saw Buckwheat, they both treated each other with respect, and all was well. Buckwheat died in the summer of 2016. She did form quite a good relationship with Jenny, and Jenny protected the yard from other cats entering. She never chased Buckwheat again, and since her passing, Jenny and Fuzzball have become quite good friends. Well, it's something Jenny tolerates and Fuzzy enjoys. Whenever Jenny is outside, Fuzzball will constantly follow her around the yard. And Jenny will occasionally chase the cat for short distances just to remind her who is in charge. She never did that to Buckwheat.

What I learned from this is that we must all learn to deal with those who are different from us. We must all learn to love our neighbor, even if they are not someone with whom we might want to hang out, or even someone who thinks differently than we do on just about everything.

Jesus reminded us of the same thing in the parable of the Good Samaritan. It's found in Luke 10:25–37. A lawyer asked Jesus about salvation, and the lawyer was attempting to catch Him in some violation of the law, so he could accuse Jesus of something. But Jesus turned the tables on him and asked him how he thought salvation was obtained. The lawyer said, "You know, love God with all your heart and love your neighbor as yourself." Jesus said he got it right. Then the lawyer wanted a little more. Being a lawyer, he wanted some clarification, some little bit of guidance on how to utilize this for practical purposes. So he asked Jesus, "Who is my neighbor?"

> *Then Jesus answered and said: "A certain man went down from Jerusalem to Jericho, and fell among thieves, who stripped him of his clothing, wounded him, and departed, leaving him half dead. Now by chance a certain priest came down that road. And when he saw him, he passed by on the other side.*
>
> *Likewise a Levite, when he arrived at the place, came and looked, and passed by on the other side. But a certain Samaritan, as he journeyed, came where he was. And when he saw him, he had compassion. So he went to him and bandaged his wounds, pouring on oil and wine; and he set him on his own animal, brought him to an inn, and took care of him. On the next day, when he departed, he took out two denarii, gave them to the innkeeper, and said to him, 'Take care of him; and whatever more you spend, when I come again, I will repay you.' So which of these three do you think was neighbor to him who fell among the thieves?"*
>
> *And he said, "He who showed mercy on him." Then Jesus said to him, "Go and do likewise."*

This display of love was godly love, not this man's. For man's love is always incomplete. God's love is complete. When we show love, not our love but God's love, to anyone else but especially to those who are different— even those who may believe very differently, who may look differently, those who may be foul smelling and worse acting, those who may never even thank you and, in fact, may even do damage to your property, your emotional stability, and your being—we are reinforcing the greatest display of love ever offered to the world. It's the love from the cross by Jesus.

DAVID ROSS SHERMAN

How can we share the Gospel of Christ, this good news that is given so freely by God to the world, if we fail to show His love to those whom we present it? The short answer is that we can't —at least not logically. The mind cannot accept hypocrisy when it detects it. When we discover someone who says one thing but does something quite different and in opposition to what he has said, we rebel. We stand up. We admonish. We shout it out. We post it on Facebook. (Although please don't believe everything you read on Facebook.)

In the confrontation between Jenny and Buckwheat, there was no ambiguity, no pretense, no diplomatic maneuvering, and no hypocrisy. There was a very short introduction, and then there was forever peace.

When we live our lives with the fullness of love in our heart, then we will soon discover that from that heart of love, we will take actions that will produce great outpourings of love and yield rewards for both receiver and giver. We will speak words that will offer both comfort and compassion for those we know and love and with whom we agree and those we don't. And most importantly, our thoughts will turn to genuine concern that we are always displaying a love representative of the King of heaven, so we will never fail in completely loving our neighbor, no matter who they may be.

CHAPTER TWELVE

I'm All about Relationship

LIFE AS A human is all about relationship. All the time and with everything. It is the same with animals and often, as you have seen in this book, between species. Humans and dogs and cats and birds and even plants, we must all get along. We must all relate. Now granted, some of those relationships we have are fleeting, such as a waitress or waiter or the guy at the drive-through window, while others are more intense and require more time and more of your energy dedicated to the relationship.

This is the relationship with Jenny. Since she is dedicating nearly all her time and most of her energy to me, she expects a lot of the same from me as well. My wife sometimes expresses a bit of jealousy at our relationship, but I have only to say, "Jenny waits outside my shop in the snow until I exit rather than be in the midst of the noise or too far from me by being in the house. Would you?" She has never given me an answer, and I have never pressed for one. I think that strategy is wise.

But that's what Jenny taught me about relationships. Sometimes the reward of having a friend who will give you comfort when you need it, will provide you sustenance when required, and will just be there when you are in need of anything is worth a little time of discomfort or inconvenience. That friend will be there when your need is great or even when it is small. That friend will bring you love.

As we experience life with all its mountaintops and valleys, with the difficult and the sublime, we must, or at least we should, consider not only our relationship with the events and people and places we can see and experience within those events but also with those things unseen—those things that may be moving situations and people in ways not understood by physical means. There are many who fail to discover the unseen and many who cannot see beyond this physical plane, this three-dimensional world, and that is an extremely sad situation, for those people will create all their productivity and discovery here and now rather than enjoy an eternity of producing and discovering the good that only flows from God.

We get out of any relationship what we put into it, and the most exciting part is when both parties in a relationship put all their energy and all of themselves into the relationship. If done in a manner that is unselfish and giving, it will result in both parties experiencing the best possible result.

You might wonder how you could have a relationship with an event, but if you really consider your entire life, it is all about each event that has happened at various times throughout your life and the emotions that are born from those memories. I was honored to serve for two weeks at ground zero at the World Trade Center after the attacks with The Salvation Army. No one could serve longer, unless you were from the area. My relationship with that event, like so many Americans, is one whose memory spawns anger and sadness and confusion. But for me, it is the smell. Whenever I see or hear anything to do with WTC that smell returns. It haunts me. And then the anger and sadness and confusion at why hatred murdered three thousand people returns. That is my relationship with that event. The memory of those attacks has attempted to steal my joy and remove me from the place of joy. We don't have a very good relationship.

But there are other events that happen often in life that give us much more joyful memories, and our relationships with those events are more of the type we want to nourish and bring to the forefront of our memory banks. We want to return there often. And we should. But I have learned that we should live in neither the good nor the bad memories of our past. We should dwell in the present. In the present is where we will discover what is needed, not only to nourish our earthly relationships but our spiritual relationships as well. When we dwell in the past, we are living where no change can occur. We become that thing with which we relate, and whether it is dark or whether it is light, it is not now, and it changes nothing for good at all.

I believe it is always good to have a memory, for the events of our past are what have made us who we are. And actually, it is not the event itself but our relationship with the event, our perception, and our thoughts regarding that event that have made us who we are. And our spirituality has everything to do with that.

I have worked as a hospital chaplain. I have stood at the bedside of people who have passed from this life to the next. In fact, I stood at the bedside as my own mother passed from this life. I sang over and over again the twenty-third Psalm for she loved it. Suddenly her eyes opened. She reached out her arms as if to be lifted up by someone, and then she drew her last breath. I don't know what she saw, but it seemed to excite her. It was good. I have been next to some people who have no relationship with God as they pass, and it is a very different experience.

As our relationship with God becomes stronger, it overflows into every facet of our lives (and even death). It allows us to look at life in a more complete way. It enables us to understand what it is to know of an eternity without strife and disappointment and to look forward to peace and life without pain. But even here, even now, we will, if we are committed to our relationship with God, enjoy a very much enhanced relationship with everything else—our family, our friends, strangers, and most of all, our memories.

We are able to keep our relationship with our God strong in only one way. We must give it value. For those things we value, we visit often. We embrace the totality of the relationship. Jenny follows me around all the time and is never far from me. God is even closer. I surely like that. In fact, look at this:

Acts 17:26–28

> *And He has made from one blood every nation of men to dwell on all the face of the earth, and has determined their pre-appointed times and the boundaries of their dwellings, so that they should seek the Lord, in the hope that they might grope for Him and find Him, though He is not far from each one of us; for in Him we live and move and have our being, as also some of your own poets have said, "For we are also His offspring."*

Without God, we are unable to even draw breath. That is pretty intense, don't you think? Someone so very close to us should not be difficult to find. Yet each of us has gone through a period in our lives in which we were tried and perhaps tested. If our relationship with God is in pretty good shape, it will have survived the trial or test. But even if it is not strong when the test begins, it is possible that it will be made stronger if we, as we pass through the difficulty, cry out to God, for He has promised to answer if we call.

The relationship Jenny and I have is one of not only mutual care and love for one another but one of loyalty and respect for each other's presence. I enjoy that a great deal, but imagine having that with God if you can.

To be with God—to spend time with Him in very real ways, recognizing just who He is and knowing that He is with you every moment and has promised to never leave you or forsake you—should bring you great peace. I know it does for me. In fact, there are many promises made by God in His Word that we should all seek out and study because each one is a building block in our relationship with Him. They each are intended to grow both our faith and our trust in Him. As we grow in faith with God, we grow in our relationship because faith is the basis, the foundation, for all other things in God.

A good relationship is one that always expands and grows. When it stops growing and building, it becomes stagnant and still. In my relationship with my wife, we each attempt to make surprises for one another that bring joy and laughter, for it keeps our relationship in harmony. We have stressful jobs that can often cause problems within a marriage, so it is good to remove the stress from each other by just doing some simple things that we know the other will enjoy. They need not be expensive, but they do need to be considerate and kind.

God gives us that through His Word, for it is always bringing new things to us from each passage. I have read some of the same verses again and again, wandering the depth of a passage, contemplating the wonders of what it may mean, and examining each word as it is laid out on the page; and I always, without exception, walk away enriched by those new things I have discovered in those words.

I am pretty sure Paul felt the same way when he wrote this in Ephesians 3:14–19:

> *For this reason I bow my knees to the Father of our Lord Jesus Christ, from whom the whole family in heaven and earth is named, that He would grant you, according to the riches of His glory, to be strengthened with might through His Spirit in the inner man, that Christ may dwell in your*

hearts through faith; that you, being rooted and grounded
in love, may be able to comprehend with all the saints what
is the width and length and depth and height—to know
the love of Christ which passes knowledge; that you may be
filled with all the fullness of God.

Each time we add something from God into our hearts and let it linger there and fill us with all the wisdom and love that is so present within the Lord and can be released within each of us, we enter into His Word and let it grow within us. After all, His Word is described as living and powerful.

Hebrews 4:12

For the word of God is living and powerful, and sharper
than any two-edged sword, piercing even to the division
of soul and spirit, and of joints and marrow, and is a
discerner of the thoughts and intents of the heart.

If God is able to impart life to words, how much more can He do for you and me? Until we dive into His Word and totally immerse ourselves within that same word, though, we will be stuck where we are in our relationship with Him.

Jenny shows me newness quite often. She follows me around all the time and seeks what new thing I may have for her. She also seeks the comfort of my presence. I seek comfort from her presence as well, for she always brings me joy when she is near and shows me affection. She loves to learn, and I do think she feels a sense of accomplishment when she does learn something new. When I reward her with a, "Good girl, Jenny!" I see her brighten in a way that is difficult to explain. But it is pure joy. It is the tail-wagging, excited kind of joy that is able to speak volumes, all without words.

I think God enjoys our presence as well. I know that He is pleased when we are able to overcome some of the small things that haunt each of us. He is overjoyed when He sees us conquer the big things, like illnesses, that may be present but not controlling our actions as we continue to praise Him during the trial, all the while keeping our faith that He will bring us through it. And the same can be said for each trial, tribulation, or temptation we may face. And we should also maintain that extreme joy at knowing that our Master is well pleased at our joy and our excitement at that victory over the tough things. So is your tail wagging yet?

CHAPTER THIRTEEN

Bath Time

S OME DOGS JUST hate baths. Some really like them a lot. I have had both. Jenny doesn't really hate a bath, but getting her into the bathroom is sometimes a hilarious event. She seems to know when it's bath time, and I haven't quite been able to figure out how she does it. I must walk differently or something. But when I head toward the bathroom, which is not an unusual event, but only when I have it in mind to bathe her, she will begin to crouch down and walk that walk of shame a dog walks when it knows it has done something wrong. You know the one. One of my kids did that too, and she always wondered how we knew it was her that had done something. I wonder if she learned it from the dog.

When I say, "Want to take a bath, Jenny?" her head will turn away from me as she continues walking toward me, all crouched down and guilty. I'm pretty sure she thinks this is some punishment for her munching the cat's food, and since I grew up Catholic, I'm good with that. I was taught that any guilt can be equally applied in all situations if one thinks enough about the sin for which he should feel guilt. This makes guilt an ever-present entity in our life. I'm glad Jenny doesn't hold on to it. (I am not disparaging Catholics in any way, merely making a statement regarding my upbringing.)

Once inside the bathroom, I will run the water as she sits facing the door, in case it suddenly opens and she can make a break for it. When the water is at the right temperature, I just say, "OK," and she jumps into the tub. I use the spray from a shower wand to bathe and rinse her. She knows it is good for her. (Well, she might not know it's good for her, but I think she knows it's good, at least after a few minutes.) She begins each time to relax and will even lift her front paws so her underside is more easily obtained. It is amusing to watch the transition each time from guilt and apprehension to acceptance to enjoyment—every time.

It reminds me of how I am with God, perhaps you as well. I am so overcome with guilt as a result of sin that I stay away from Him, even though I know and fully understand that He loves me and would never do harm to me. Once I remember how much He loves me, even to the point of suffering in my place and dying for me, and I recall the reason for His sacrifice, then I move toward Him for there is no fear in me anymore. The fear I had was overcome by love because love is a much more powerful emotion. And there is no power greater in the universe than the power of God's love—for me, for you, for all His creation, but especially for us who have been given a soul.

We must never fear God if we are one of His children. We must learn to do what He asks for He is full of mercy. Psalm 136 declares twenty-six times that His mercy endures forever. That's a long time. He is very patient, but that does not excuse our eventual learning of what must be learned: that we should love God with all our heart and love our neighbors as ourselves. All our heart- that's a lot. But it's what He does for each of us for He has given us life. That's a lot. And He offers us life that will last forever—never-ending life with no pain or suffering. That's a lot. When we choose to love God with all our heart, which means acting as though He were present in every situation and choosing to do His will simply because it is His will even if it goes against our will, then we are doing a lot to show that we love God with all our heart. When we go out of our way to help someone else in his need, even when it is difficult, without complaining and without resistance to the leading of the Holy Spirit, then we are doing a lot to show that we love our neighbor. But it is only what we are supposed to do.

When we sin, we fail to love God with all our heart or love our neighbor as ourselves because all sin is either against God or a neighbor. So sin is failure. That's why the word interpreted as *sin* in the Bible means "to miss the mark." But it doesn't mean that it is a terminal failure. Because God's mercy endures forever, we are welcomed back home into His love again and again, and He patiently works with each of us, as long as we are trying. Just keep in mind that the second part of the definition of the word means "to not share in the victory because you have missed the mark."

Jenny goes dutifully to the bath in spite of some mistaken fear that grips her, possibly from some past event or perhaps just a personality quirk that prevents her from getting excited about such things as baths, but she need never fear that I will punish her in a cruel fashion. She knows that in her heart. But somewhere, she was either mistreated, or she misinterpreted some action. And now she possesses an inexplicable fear, embedded deep within her heart. Fear the bath, fear many things, but never fear the master. I am convinced that the reason she doesn't run and hide when bath is anticipated is because it is I who stand at the door. Even though she has no desire to enter the bathroom, she does because she knows that no harm will ever come to her while I am there. That kind of comfort is worth a lot when it comes to overcoming fear. When the one who stands in the place that *should* cause fear is the one who provides food and shelter for you, protects you, teaches you, leads you, and loves you, then fear can take a long walk off a short pier. You know it will be OK.

God is exactly all those things. I can't think of anything He doesn't do on that list, not just for me but for all of us, if we allow Him. We should not fear if we believe in our hearts that He is where we are going. That does take some practice simply because if you have not done it on a regular basis, you have been trusting the wrong person—yourself.

When I lived in the throes and control of the world, the choices I made were always wrong. Sometimes it was my own desires that caused the problem, and sometimes it was because I trusted the wrong advice; either way, it was my choice. I have found that if you always look to the agenda of those who give advice, then you will know how to discern that advice. Whose interests do they defend? Where do they lead? Do not seek godly advice from the ungodly. They have a completely different viewpoint on everything. In fact, I don't think I would seek *any* advice from the ungodly. Apparently, someone else did as well.

Psalms 1:1–3

> *Blessed is the man Who walks not in the counsel of the ungodly, Nor stands in the path of sinners, Nor sits in the seat of the scornful; But his delight is in the law of the Lord, And in His law he meditates day and night. He shall be like a tree Planted by the rivers of water, That brings forth its fruit in its season, Whose leaf also shall not wither; And whatever he does shall prosper.*

DAVID ROSS SHERMAN

This psalm is an introduction to the book of Psalms. The book is a how-to book for knowing the Lord, written by some people who understood aspects of God we probably do not. But mainly, it shows us how to learn to trust the Lord in ways we had not considered before. In fact, I think that's what the Bible is intended to do in its entirety. It is the book of *re's*. You know, repent, renew, restore, but mainly reconsider. That is what makes God available to everyone. But since He is God, He is the one who gets to determine the rules. And He lays them out quite clearly in His Word. There can be no mistake, and there is but one way in which we may approach God. He has put all His power in the only Son He ever had, Jesus. That is why we are able to do the same.

Jenny has put her trust in me—full and complete trust. She is never far from me, and when I ask of her something that is not really what she desires to do, she will reluctantly do it. I understand that sometimes direction from the Lord is unclear and difficult to see, but that is when we should wait. My direction to Jenny is very clear, at least to me, but when she misjudges my intentions for her, I try to understand that she does not understand. God does the same with us. He will take steps to correct our direction but only if we seek Him and seek that direction. It would be the same with me if Jenny did not seek to understand whatever it was I was attempting to teach her. If she walks away and doesn't even attempt to learn, then there is nothing I can do to teach her. If she maintained that same attitude, I would still love her. I would even continue taking care of her, but I would no longer attempt to teach her new things, at least for a while. When we cease from seeking knowledge of God, we cease growing in our relationship for the relationship is suddenly one-sided. God already knows everything about any and all of us, so we should seek all we can of Him in order that our lives will be filled with truth and knowledge of the most caring and loving being in the universe.

It can be quite difficult because we are very busy people. If we become so busy we never come to the point where we do actually seek after Him, we are lost for eternity. And yet we may reluctantly seek God in our lives and come to the point where we are believers but never move from that stage. That is all right for a short while, but we should, at some point, come to the understanding that being a lukewarm Christian is as bad as being an unbeliever. It has the same ending. To experience God at all, you must experience Him entirely. And to experience Him entirely, you must begin to seek and to walk through the bathroom door, discarding your fears in the hall as you enter into the peace of your Master. He will never do harm to you for He loves you. But in order to feel that serene peace and joy, knowing that He is there with you in any situation that may be unpeaceful and anything but serene, you need only to cry out to Him. Uttering the name of Jesus in any situation may not bring you into His full presence immediately, but it will bring you into the beginnings of an awareness of His presence. He is always there with you, so you need not ask Him to show up. You just may not be aware of His presence.

There are many ways in which we may bring ourselves into that awareness, and speaking His name is only one. You should pray to God to show you how He would like to speak with you, and then do it often. Once Jenny has jumped into the tub and begins to feel the warm water wash over her, she relaxes and allows me to rub shampoo into her, and she seems to enjoy it. It is a strange experience, not an everyday thing, but once the misplaced fear has been replaced with the knowledge of the truth, all is well. We can do the same. We have nothing to fear from God. He always has mercy and grace for us. But He desires that we actually walk through the door toward Him, and that door is Jesus.

DAVID ROSS SHERMAN

CHAPTER FOURTEEN

Will You Please Just Touch Me?

IN THE FIRST week after I had adopted Jenny, as I opened the door to the church building, Jenny ran ahead of me; and about four feet into the chapel, she rolled over on her back, exposing her tummy to the ceiling and began writhing back and forth. I began to laugh, and she continued to rock back and forth, looking like an eel who had been thrown on the bank or a turtle trapped in his overturned shell and wiggling his feet, that is, until I touched her. She instantly froze and waited for the caress, which I felt she trusted would be both continual and gentle.

She reminded me of an alligator who was calmed from the gentle stroking of its underside. As other people came through the door, she began to do that in front of every person. But rather than wonder if my dog had lost her mind, each one exhibited exactly the same reaction, reaching down to give a little rub to the upturned tummy, so Jenny was effectively able to communicate her desire to every person who entered.

That isn't always easy, making others understand what we want or even what we need. Communication is often difficult among us humans, and we have language. Sometimes I think it would be easier if we would just roll over and wiggle on the floor. I know sometimes that I feel like doing that, but I'm afraid of being arrested.

Here's the secret to success in the world of communication. It's one of the lines from the prayer known as the prayer of St. Francis. It states, "Let me seek not so much to be consoled as to console, / To be understood as to understand, / To be loved as to love . . ." What a beautiful sentiment. If we could do that to every person we meet, we could fix world peace in a day.

I won't hold my breath.

But here's the thing. If we learn to look for those who need consoling or understanding or love, we will discover that we are being consoled or understood or loved by everyone. As we reach out to touch others in love, we will have our own needs fulfilled, and we will discover a peace that invades every situation.

Jenny figured that out all by herself. She is so generous with her love that everyone wants to share it with her. By giving in generous amounts, she receives it in generous amounts. And she seems to understand fully that is how it works.

Now granted, lying on one's back and writhing like a living hot dog may not be appealing to everyone, but those who don't know the joy of a good belly rub just don't know what they don't know. Jenny is so filled with an inner joy that she wants to share it with everyone, except other dogs. She really likes to be the top dog around humans, especially me. I have a friend who has a chocolate Lab named Faith. Faith is a bit larger than Jenny, and Faith and I have a good relationship. She is a very loving dog toward humans as well, especially to me it seems because I give it back to her. Most ignore her save a quick brush.

When Faith is around, she tries to push Jenny away from me, and Jenny will allow it, to an extent. Faith is in no way aggressive, and Jenny has some female aggression issues, so I was amazed to see her capitulate to Faith. They do play well together, a bit rough, so I see Jenny's return to warrior status a little bit. But they both know when to stop. That's the problem with us who do not wear fur naturally. We don't know when to stop. That's the part of the process with which we always seem to have the greatest difficulty. James figured it out like this:

James 1:14–15

> But each one is tempted when he is drawn away by his own desires and enticed. Then, when desire has conceived, it gives birth to sin; and sin, when it is full-grown, brings forth death.

That little phrase "when desire has conceived" is where we should have stopped. Our own desires draw us away so easily into sin and into things that will not matter. God has a plan for you, for me, and for everyone. But we must acknowledge Him as who He is in order to access that plan.

When Jenny submits to my will, our relationship is strengthened, and she always submits to my will (eventually) because I have given her nothing but love. Sometimes that love comes in discipline but never involves striking her or violence. I teach her the way her mother taught her. I am aware of everything she does simply because she is with me all the time. So she trusts my judgment for her and knows that I have her best interests in mind.

When we submit to God's will, the rewards are staggering. By submitting to God's will for our lives, we must understand that we are saying we are aware that God has awareness of our lives—our every thought, word, and deed. And because He does, we have but to follow His direction in whatever situation that happens, and we will experience the fullest and best-possible experience in that situation.

And this process will never involve sin or darkness. It will always involve one of nine things—love, joy, peace, patience, kindness, goodness, faithfulness, gentleness, or self-control. A situation entered into by means of the direction of God will be resolved by the use of one or more of these things. Or it is possible that one may be achieved by the exercise of another. For example, peace is obtained by utilizing self-control, or perhaps joy is achieved by kindness. The possibilities are endless combinations, and they are always present in godly people. That's how you know they're godly people. That is why Paul referred to these things as the fruits of the Spirit.

Jenny knows people pretty well. I am fairly certain there is a smell or energy attributed to darkness, and most animals are able to detect it. I have learned to trust the instincts of several animals I have had. I have seen Jenny stand away from certain people, and I do as well when it happens. Dogs are good that way. We call it discernment. Jenny has taught me to give everyone the opportunity to be loved in the way they deserve. She offers her tummy, and if someone passes it by, the opportunity of a lifetime, to receive love, is missed, then so be it. Just move on to someone who actually wants that kind of love. The act itself is an act of submission, but to Jenny, it's more than that. It's how she lets people know that it's all right to submit. It can be done in a loving way. No need to be embarrassed, and no need to be offended—just submit, receive a rub, and move on . . . next!

God is like that too. Jesus won't force anyone to love Him. I don't really understand why anyone would not love Him, but then again, I was in that bunch for many years, so I know it can happen. There's a great gnawing that begins deep within your soul, and if you allow it to rise and you begin to seek what it is, truth will inevitably give invitation to accept it. If anyone refuses, there may be another gnawing—another opportunity to accept that same truth, but then again, there may not be. It's like the line from Julius Caesar:

There is a tide in the affairs of men.

Which, taken at the flood, leads on to fortune;

Omitted, all the voyage of their life

Is bound in shallows and in miseries.

If you substitute the words *salvation* for *fortune* and *eternity* for *life*, you have the story of salvation.

We are only permitted to enjoy our eternity if we walk through the door of Jesus and let Him rub our tummies. Seize the opportunity when it is presented. The unfailing love that is like no other is at hand, but it is up to each of us to begin the search for the truth of that love. When we live in the world of distractions and falsehoods, we must expect to experience distrust and deceit. That is the way of the world, after all.

What we see from Jesus is the experience of love in its highest form for it is the kind of love that gives all it can and never asks for anything in return. For the gift God gives, He has already given, and it can be no more. It is the gift of His only Son, Jesus. This sacrifice of His life on an instrument of death has given life to all who will humble themselves and walk into the light of His love. It is the most important thing we can do in this life for it is the doorway to eternal life, and there is but one. If we just touch Him, we will understand the fullness of that love. It may not be an easy path, and in fact, I can almost guarantee it won't, but the reward of being able to live now in the presence of God and to learn to share in those things to which He directs you is certainly worth the trials and tribulations you may encounter or the temptations you must learn to overcome. It is in these things we discover the truth about love, for the love God offers us touches us daily and assists us as we touch others with that same love.

CHAPTER FIFTEEN

I Will Always Be by Your Side

ONE OF THE fruits of the Spirit is faithfulness. It is a pretty important one for it speaks to loyalty. Not loyalty alone but it is probably the biggest component. Most dogs are pretty faithful, and that is a good thing, but I have seen a few who are only chasing some food. They work on someone's heart to gain a meal and are gone with first light—cheaters.

Jenny doesn't have that problem. Part of training is developing loyalty to the one who issues commands, and the dog must know that the person who is issuing those commands is the leader. If the person does not command the respect of the animal, the training will fail. But Jenny seems to transcend that relationship of dog and trainer and move to a relationship that seems more of a friendship in which one friend asks another to do something and that friend responds in the affirmative, like church pickups.

I have a friend whom I pastor, and I pick him up every Sunday for church. Jenny rides in the passenger seat on the way. When I pull up to his house, she will look at me, and when I tip my head toward the back seat or grunt, she will jump back there and wait for him to get into the vehicle. As soon as his arm hits the armrest between the seats, she dives nose first into the crux of his arm in order to give him a hug. When he begins to giggle, she will look up and begin to lick his face as much as he will allow. She has a special affinity for this particular friend, and she does that particular action with only one other person, my wife, Tina.

Jenny is faithful to perform this action every single time when either of them is in the vehicle, but so far, she has done it for no one else. But she knows a lot about people, and I am unsure how. It may be their smell, or it may be their actions, or it may be the sounds they make, perhaps a rise in blood pressure or some other thing. But this I know: she knows when people need a hug, she can tell me if there is some questionable person about, and she is quick to respond if someone seems to be upset or in trouble. She is very faithful to perform these actions, but usually, she will wait for me to tell her it's all right to go for her first loyalty is to me. That is not always true, and there are only two exceptions: if someone is in visible distress, Jenny will be at that person's side, and if he has cheese, Jenny will be at that person's side. Most know not to indulge her, but some have succumbed to the big brown eyes.

If we were to look at our relationship with God in the same way, we might discover that if we place our loyalty to God first and wait until He puts all the pieces in place for us to move forward in any situation, whether that situation is to help someone else or to help ourselves, as we wait in anticipation to do whatever is in our hearts to do, we can be faithfully preparing our heart as well as doing other things necessary to accomplish the mission.

That preparation should be a time of prayer and perhaps even fasting. I am pretty sure Jenny will never go through a fast. She gets pretty anxious if she misses one meal, but we are not like that. Well, we have the capability to overcome our desire for food at least for a while—some people a week, some a day, some a meal. The idea behind fasting is simple. You deny your flesh in order to get more in touch with your spirit. Many religions have fasting as one of their tenets, and denial of self is not unique to Christianity. In fact, in some Christian denominations and churches, self-indulgence is more the norm.

We must become faithful to do what we can do in order to please our Master. Jenny has learned that if she is faithful to me and does the things I ask, she understands that I will be faithful to take care of her. What she doesn't know is that I will do that anyway. It doesn't matter what she does, but it will be difficult to take care of her if she leaves me, if she runs away, if she even drifts out of my view for a short period. But it doesn't happen. Whether she is protecting me or needs my protection, we both feel better when we're in each other's company, so why not just be in each other's company? Neither of us seems to care why we like each other, and we have never discussed it. It's just the way it is.

When we walk away from God, we should probably expect to suffer some consequences and some do, but the difference between Jenny running away from me and someone running away from God are eternal. If you do well in this life, owning fame and fortune to whatever degree to impress yourself sufficiently but you have no relationship with

God, then you are, of all people, to be pitied. For the fleeting nature of worldly goods are surely a draw to the young and ambitious, but for those who are able to discern the world of the spirit, seeing light for light and darkness for darkness, the trappings of shiny things are not only offensive but repugnant and not attractive at all. Aside from the obvious technological uses needed to navigate society today, simplicity, as much as is possible, is certainly a less complicated way to live our lives, but it will also assist us in being faithful to those things we should while developing habits that assist us in being faithful in all areas of our lives.

I have thought about what it would be like to be Jenny—to have lived her life; to have been rejected by everyone you thought you could love and who should have loved you; to have been offered a way out only to find out that it wasn't real, but was only temporary; then to be put in a cage for a long time and then rescued for the last time, forever.

That is my story too (except for the cage part), and if it isn't your story, then it can be. But you have to figure that out for yourself. Jenny's life, for the rest of her life, will be one that is filled with love and friendship of a master she loves and who loves her, unless I die before her. That's the problem with human masters; they all go away. None of us gets out of here alive. But if I am allowed to spend the rest of my days with Jenny by my side, then she will have finished well. I hope I can finish as well as her.

But it is different for those of us who have the power of thought, the power of free will, and the power to choose. That's why faithfulness for humans is so valued. Animals are faithful to a master because the master feeds them or takes care of them. With God, He is faithful to us, even when we are not faithful to Him. He is able to do this because He can see the end of things (around the corner, if you will), and because of this, He is able to be causal when it comes to our lives. He can put us on the path of whatever may be needed in order to progress to the next level of a relationship with us. And make no mistake, God desires a relationship with us—each one of us. And He desires the relationship to be one of mutual affection. He loves us enough to allow His only begotten Son to suffer and die and then be brought back to life so He could spend eternity with me and you. That's true love. But we often act as though we deserve such a thing, and we expect God to reward us for just being in His presence when it is us who should be seeking what we can do for God as we enter into His presence.

The evidence that Jenny desires to be in my presence is that she is in my presence. She is faithful to seek my presence. As I write this, she lies across the doorway to my office so that, should I leave the room, she will be disturbed and be able to follow me wherever I go in the house. And if I go outside, she will follow. We are having a wind advisory here today. We are experiencing "fifty miles per hour" wind gusts with sustained winds of thirty to forty miles per hour. Jenny hates the wind and will do most anything to stay out of it, but if I open the door to walk outside, she will follow me, just because she will be with me. If I go into my shop, she will not follow because of the loud noises and bad smells, but she will wait outside, on the walk, until I come out. Wind, rain, or snow, it doesn't matter. She wants to be near me.

I have sometimes fooled her in order to get her out of the weather while I work out in the shop. I will run back into the house, and when I open the door for her to run inside, I turn around and head back to my shop. When I do return to the house, she will be lying by the front door, awaiting my return with her tail wagging as she welcomes me back into her presence while she moves back into the comfort of mine.

Jenny has taught me the reality of faithfulness. I had not experienced such faithfulness, either in giving or receiving. And that is certainly my own fault. We all have the same ability to demand more of ourselves as far as our effort toward making others happy and being faithful to those we should have loved, but too often (and as is the case with yours truly), the decisions we make without God in our lives to influence those decisions are most often very bad ones, and they may cause severe damage to those we should have loved. These are not things we are or of which we should be proud of, but if they are in your past, as they are in mine, then there is nothing that can be done to change them. We can only plead for forgiveness and move on with our lives. Some are successful at this, and some are not.

Faithfulness to the future demands that we erase the pain of our past from our memory and live in the dreams and aspirations of our future, not in a passive way but rather actively involved in the process of making what God has put in our heart become reality. And if, for whatever reason, we fail to include God in the process, then we will undoubtedly make decisions that will lead to an ungodly conclusion. We began the dream at hope and have put our faith in something, be it seen or unseen. If we have been so fortunate as to have obtained hope, then we owe loyalty to that person, place, or thing that has brought us out of the pain and into that hope.

If it is God that has given you hope, then I suggest you pursue God with all the energy you have. If it is something else, consider this: this thing or person or entity in which you trust, what does it offer regarding eternity? And does the eternity it offers come by means of love, or does it come in anger? Does its eternity have peace, and has it offered mercy and compassion? And is it for everyone who wants to be there? God alone, through His only Son Jesus, offers such a place, and everyone is welcome. He deserves your faithfulness in every aspect of your life for He alone offers hope. Faithfulness to Him is really not that difficult once you understand He is like no one you ever knew . . . ever. He is a faithful Master, and His desire for you is that you become an obedient child.

Jenny has hope that her next meal is provided without much difficulty, and she also owns faith that it will happen. Her hope comes through a conditioning process and not through anything she has learned. For as much as some want to believe that dogs are as smart as humans, they really don't have much understanding of deep and eternal matters. I hope she will be able to romp in heaven, but I really don't think that is how it works. However, God has more things planned than we mere mortals are able to imagine, so anything is possible. I hope so. For now, I know she is by my side and doesn't stray too far from there. If she is allowed, she will always be by my side. Although she will defend me to the death, she knows that I will protect her as well. And she seems to take both jobs very seriously. Her faithfulness to me and the position she always holds so very faithfully are evidence to me of how I should be with God.

If I move away from His marvelous protection by straying into darkness and away from His light, I am putting myself in danger, and I have no one to blame but myself for following either my greed, my lusts, or my selfish desires. And I take a chance of perhaps never finding my way back home, for those things that are offered by an enemy may be so delightful to our flesh but cause great and immediate harm to our spirit. And in the end, all that matters is our spirit. So we should learn to be faithful to that spirit and chase after those things that will bring our spirit joy and are the things of God.

In the same token, though, if someone speaks badly of God to me, blaming Him for things He has not done or even speaking His name in vile profanities, my first reaction is to defend Him. I am unsure that He would need defense, but even the shepherd David defended Him to a giant one day, and guess what? The giant went down. God alone is able to bring us to that place of peaceful harmony in both spirit and flesh for He alone is faithful and will always be by our side.

DAVID ROSS SHERMAN

CHAPTER SIXTEEN

I Will Be Patient with You

I AM NOT a patient person. I am a type A personality, and that does not make for patient people. I demand much of myself and believe we all should. And when I want to do something, I like to get it done, whether it is building something, moving something, cutting wood, or doing any other project that happens to lie before me.

Because of this manner of being, some people stay a distance from me. But Jenny doesn't. As I age and find myself in more and more situations where I am sitting for extended periods (such as writing this book), she is always found very near me and awaits my movement. She understands I can't or perhaps won't sit for very long, so as soon as I move, she jumps up to follow, unless I ask her to stay. She will stay for a minute or two, but if I am gone too long, she will come find me.

But she will wait for me no matter what it is I may be doing, and I believe it is for one reason. She knows that she is on my mind. Because of this, I am on hers. She understands that I am never going to leave her, so she will wait if she must. It may be challenging sometimes for it may mean sitting in the snow or in the rain, but she always does it, and she does it with great patience. The reward is her understanding of what it is to be with me. She needs no other reward for her patience. And my reward is knowing that she has given herself to the task of waiting.

I am pretty sure God feels the same way about us. If we just wait for Him as He does the things He needs to do to give us what we need in order to do whatever it is He desires we do, we will be rewarded. It is worth the wait. One of my and many other people's favorite verse is Isaiah 40:31:

> But those who wait on the Lord Shall renew their strength;
> They shall mount up with wings like eagles, They shall run
> and not be weary, They shall walk and not faint.

This speaks to waiting, but more than that, it speaks to patiently waiting. Sometimes we are made to wait, and some of us don't want to wait. So we are very impatient in our waiting. We make ourselves, as well as those around us, crazy by our discontent at having to wait for whatever it is we hope will come to pass. One of the joys of waiting for something is the reward of it actually happening. When it happens, we are able to be filled with joy at it finally happening. That which is cherished is always worth the wait.

There is an African eagle called the bateleur eagle. It is a bird that has been clocked at 125 miles per hour in a dive and is the only bird that knowingly flies upside down. No one knows why for sure, but I suspect the bird likes it. We should all learn to soar like that once in a while and maybe even fly upside down once in a while.

And as you read the words of this passage, imagine soaring at a very high rate of speed, for that's what is described by these words. A very rapid ascent, climbing ever higher, is akin to the reward from just waiting on the Lord. We are also told that those who wait on the Lord will run and not grow weary. I have personally experienced this feeling of being able to go on even when I thought it impossible to go on. In my work on disasters, with the combination of God's magic elixir called adrenaline and His Holy Spirit, I have discovered we are able to transcend what our normal ability to operate may be. Disasters are always a waiting game.

You wait for the disaster to end, you wait for a recovery team to form, you wait for enough money to heal people's difficulties (if they are uninsured), and you wait for the healing or final recovery to be completed. But the end is always the same. People soar on wings like eagles. That is able to happen only if we allow God to work a spiritual healing within us as well.

As humans, to be successful at life, we must deal with everything on four different levels—physical, mental, emotional, and spiritual. Some things don't affect one area as much as another, but all are affected by everything that happens in our lives. If we fail to address any particular area at some level, we will probably be weak in that area. I think that the most neglected area is, by far, the spiritual. Many people do not even believe in a spiritual concept, but even if they don't, their disbelief makes it no less real.

To be only concerned with one area of these four will make for a very narrowly developed person for all these areas were designed by God to make us complete. And because God is spirit, He desires we come to Him in spirit. For that to happen, we must develop that spiritual side of our nature. If we are emotionally misguided to the point of making decisions that harm either ourselves or others, or if our mental state is in disrepair, then it is quite possible that our other areas will suffer as well.

What many never realize is that when our spirit is weakened, it may affect our physical being and our mental state as well and, most certainly, our emotional well-being. Sometimes events in our lives are so powerful and leave such deep emotional gouges in our spirit and our minds and then emotional scars that never go away.

Jenny has shown me that maintaining joy in every single situation goes a long way to generating gratitude in our lives. Her life began in such a way that you might well expect that it would be short and quite uneventful. But her unique brand of joy seems to have brought her into a place of joy and comfort with her situation, no matter what that situation was. I have not known many who have been able to accomplish that.

Today we visited an assisted-care facility just to show some Jenny-style joy to some of the folks who may appreciate her kind of love. These are people with whom she must exercise her patience to a great degree. Many want to touch her simply because, as one dear lady put it, "There's just something about fur." I kind of held on to Jenny pretty tight lest that lady make a little throw or a wall hanging out of my friend. But Jenny loves the attention, and she has an opportunity to show her belly to some new friends—some of who reach down to rub her tummy, while others cannot. But all the folks she encountered were so impressed by her antics that it bubbled over into much laughter and joy. I like it when that happens, for it always seems to make Jenny feel like she's doing her job. That's another reward altogether. If only everyone would learn that a job well done is its own reward.

But it takes patience to get there. It does for Jenny, it does for me, and I'm pretty sure it does for you as well. None of us start out knowing exactly how to get to safety, to that place where we feel secure in everything. So we must learn to trust one another, our family, and especially God. For it is God alone who knows the end of things no matter which way we go. We often don't have the patience to wait for

WHAT MY DOG TAUGHT ME ABOUT JESUS   ~95~

His direction, and we strike out in so many different directions with no direction at all. We flail and swing our arms in randomness with no control because we have not taken just a small amount of time to wait.

Jenny is exactly like that. She fails to wait for direction sometimes, especially when she detects something in the air—something like cat. She wants to destroy the plunderer of her friend, Fuzzball, so she will show her excitement by standing at the door and whining in a tiny voice that is always the signal for cat awareness. Were I to open the door at that moment, she would injure herself or the door or me, so I insist she assume a calmer stature and quiet herself. Then I wait to make sure it is for real. She must focus on me and not on that thing she desires. I wait, and she calms down. I open the door, and she goes out gently.

The waiting is the most important part. It is that which shows patience. With Jenny, it is all about focus. Here's a news flash: with us, it is all about focus as well. When we are embroiled in anything—and I literally mean anything—that will require some important decisions, we may either take command of our emotions or we may allow our emotions to command us. The latter is never a good way to go. But there is one thing of which I am certain: if we focus on God while we make the decision necessary to correct our situation, we will arise victorious. If we focus on God while we are suffering and we praise Him in all things good and bad, we will discover the bad things are not so bad and the good things are better. It's a pretty amazing phenomenon.

When I am teaching Jenny something new, it requires much patience on my part, but it also requires patience on her part. Learning is one of the most difficult things for anyone, but it's all about focus. If we focus on what or who we are chasing, we will be successful. That takes a lot of focus. Jenny's focus is short-lived. She is a dog, and that is the way dogs are, unless there is a reward. Rewards keep her from being bored with whatever it is I am attempting to teach her. They help her focus.

With Jesus, it's a bit different. He is the reward we seek, and if we wait patiently for Him to show up as we are involved in that seeking process, we will always be amazed at when and where it may happen. We will learn to not be surprised, but we will always be amazed. That's because everything about God is amazing—everything. When we fail to realize the greatness of His creation and when we fail to take some time to just look around at what is happening all around us at any given moment and enjoy that which has been given us, then we will fail to

DAVID ROSS SHERMAN

thank the giver. And that is sad. For nothing we see when we look up and nothing we cannot see lest it be magnified thousands of times was first designed and then created by God, and that alone makes Him worthy of our honor and praise. But even more than that, He is the author of life—for all things that are living. The patience of God is found in the creation. Just look at it. It is amazing. I sometimes picture David, a young shepherd boy, sitting in a field with his sheep. And he was truly amazed at what he saw. The night sky lit up with millions of tiny lights all spread out against the darkness. Pretty sure that is what he was seeing when he wrote this:

Psalms 19:1

> *The heavens declare the glory of God; And the firmament shows His handiwork.*

Many people live in or near a city, and the night sky is obscured by the lights of the city. I have met many people who are always so amazed at the night sky when it becomes possible to view it with no extraneous or ambient light. The sounds they make at viewing the beauty of something that is always there is amazing in and of itself, but those are the sounds we make when we are amazed. We are a people who love to be amazed, yet so many of us refuse to patiently seek the most amazing thing of all, God. It's just that simple. And God is not difficult to find, for as I have stated elsewhere, He is everywhere.

Jenny understands that there is a master she must follow. That master will protect her, see that she has food, and keep her healthy; and she, in return, will give me what I need from her. We have a pretty good understanding of each other's needs, so it works out well. If we follow Jesus as Jenny patiently follows me, we will have a really close relationship with Jesus. Jenny patiently waits for me to move, and she follows along. She waits for me to show her many things, but she also anticipates my movements. She won't go far in that, though, unless she first looks back to seek my approval.

We should follow our Master as well. We should learn to patiently wait until He tells us to move; and when we move off, anticipating His move, we should look back before we leave Him far behind. He is patient with us to allow us that freedom, but if we patiently move forward in the protection of His presence, we will always succeed, for our success will no longer be measured the way the world measures things. Rather, we will measure all success and failure by only one measure, Jesus Christ.

DAVID ROSS SHERMAN

CHAPTER SEVENTEEN

I Know How to Relax
. . . When I Must

LEARNING TO REST is an important part of life. We all need to do it. Sometimes it may even improve our level of patience. Jenny is an expert at immediate and complete relaxation. I do believe most dogs are. But I think Jenny, who is always on, excels at this particular talent.

Jenny finds resting good for two reasons. It prepares her for when she must spring into action in her role as guardian and protector from all cats. I have, as of this writing, no knowledge of why we need protection from cats, but Jenny is positive they are up to no good. That takes rest. The other reason is that one must be prepared for when it is time to take a ride or a walk or a run on the driveway.

When I watch her rest during the day, I have noticed she rarely gets into a deep sleep. At every sound or smell that enters into her range, she will react with either a twitching ear or an opened eye to further inspect the source—always on. But at night, there is a very different story. I have seen her get into a very deep sleep that involves dreaming and much movement but with no awareness of her surroundings. I once had a Doberman that used to sleep in a chair, and she would inevitably arrive at a position with her head down on the floor while her body was still in the chair. She would always fall out onto the floor unless awakened. Dogs may have some strange sleep habits.

But we all need rest. We all have troubles, and we need respite from those same troubles. It really doesn't matter what it is, whether financial, family, relationships, illness, or some sin in our lives. We all need rest from the burdens we bear and the things we suffer—some more than others, and some *much* more than others. And whether we are reposing in restless slumber like the daytime Jenny or whether we sleep so hard we fall from our rest in a violent awakening, we need some relief, some exit, from the pains we suffer in our lives.

There is only one place of which I am aware where we may find such rest—in the arms of Jesus. He made an offer to all who are suffering and in any kind of pain. It's found in Matthew 11:28–30:

> *Come to Me, all you who labor and are heavy laden, and I will give you rest. Take My yoke upon you and learn from Me, for I am gentle and lowly in heart, and you will find rest for your souls. For My yoke is easy and My burden is light.*

The words for *labor* and *heavy laden* are words that indicate someone who is just worn out and overburdened. And the word interpreted as *rest* really means "to be refreshed." Even though we may be under great pressures in our lives, and even if we may be in a place of suffering, there is always One who will offer us comfort and relief from that which we suffer. I really don't know how to explain why it is the way it is or even how it feels to have this type of relief, but I have experienced it myself, so I know it to be real. I have been so overburdened at one point that I was nearly broken. And when I ran to Jesus, when I joined with Him in my spirit, I found the strength to face that which lay before me.

You see, the word *yoke* is a word that means "to join two things." That's what a yoke does. When we take on the yoke of Christ, we are able to be joined to Him in a manner we may experience with no one else. We are able to learn from Him, directly from Him. Think about that, learning from the King of Kings. But in order to do that, we must take on His yoke, and we must be joined to Him. And what is even more important in this learning process is what we are to learn— gentleness and humility. It is in this process of becoming gentle and kind and humble that we will become one with Him and will learn to either accept our pain and suffering or overcome it. But in either case, we will praise God for what He has done.

The bar that stretches across a scale and holds the two trays, which hold that which is to be weighed as well as the weights for exacting that balance, is also called a yoke. As we are joined to Christ through, first, our seeking and then His teaching as we learn, we also learn to balance our spiritual and physical lives, while at the same time, striking balance

DAVID ROSS SHERMAN

with our emotional and mental states. These should all be weighed against that rock—that weight we call Jesus. And that is exactly what happens when we do form such a close relationship with Him. There's balance in all areas of our lives.

Jenny has learned to rest near me, and for some reason, I am unable to understand why she finds resting near me much more comforting than if she is away. She always finds where I am and makes sure I will have to trip over her to pass from my position. This way she is alerted to my exiting from wherever I may be and can follow me. I have never stepped over her, even using the stealthiest procedures I can employ, without awakening her to my movement.

Oh, that we will be awakened when we spot God moving away from us. (We are actually the one doing the moving.) And we will rise to follow Him no matter what is happening. I'm afraid that our greatest trials move us toward Him in ways we never will when we know all is well and running smooth. It is no wonder that most people discover more of God as they suffer than when the waves have stilled and the storm is no more. God's greatest desire is for us, for our success in every situation, but He knows the greatest thing we could possibly have in our lives is Him. So the best thing He is able to do for us is to allow something that will bring us near Him, perhaps even cry out to Him. If you are experiencing something of this magnitude, perhaps God is speaking to you and attempting to help you to listen to Him. My advice would be to turn your ear toward Him as well as your heart.

I am always overjoyed when I see Jenny follow me around, inside or outside. She shows her desire to just be with me when she does that, and as soon as I land someplace, she will lie down somewhere nearby and just wait. And as she waits, she will relax and wait for me to either move or ask her to come. She is extremely well versed at that, and I think she feels, as though she thinks when I rise, that we are off together for another adventure—perhaps a ride, perhaps a walk—and it really doesn't matter for she knows she will be with me and it will be good. In fact, I think Jenny feels that no matter what we are doing, it is good just because we are together. I know I feel that way, and perhaps I am merely projecting, but I always think that if she doesn't want to follow me around and be everywhere I am, she will not do it.

I hate to say it, but I am a little jealous of my dog's behavior. I desire to be close to my Master, but I often involve myself in behavior that is far from Him. So I know that, in a split second, I can leave His presence, not because He suddenly ran off somewhere but rather because I did when I chose to walk away from Him. No, God won't follow us around like a puppy, but rather, He is always there with us. We don't leave His presence but, instead, the awareness of His presence. And that is just as bad, for when we are not aware of Him, we are tempted to do things we would not do otherwise. We are tempted to sin. James is pretty sure we don't really need help to sin, such as being tempted by the devil, but we are able to do it by ourselves.

James 1:14–16

> *But each one is tempted when he is drawn away by his own desires and enticed. Then, when desire has conceived, it gives birth to sin; and sin, when it is full-grown, brings forth death. Do not be deceived, my beloved brethren.*

The thing we never consider is that sin is very unnerving, especially for those who may be in need of a restful option. But rest happens only if you are in Christ, for if you have no relationship with Jesus, then sin will have no effect on you at all, other than to make your flesh feel comfortable. But if you are a child of the King, having sin in your life will not only be unnerving but your spirit will also rise up against you, even while you are involved in whatever sin it is in which you have engaged. The Holy Spirit will not allow a sinner rest, for your conscience will be pricked and your sadness at causing your Father pain will overwhelm you. And you will be brought to your knees, probably in tears, as you contemplate what you may have done. This is the opposite of restful. This is the very antithesis of restful. It can cause some to have ulcers or other medical malfunctions because they don't know how to come back to God once they have entered into some sinful encounter. God welcomes sinners. God welcomes sinners back. I do believe He desires that we get it and that we understand, at some point, what sin does to our soul. But He is willing to forgive . . . and forget. The key, though, to not returning to this altar of forgiveness (at least as often) is to keep our eyes focused on Jesus—in every waking moment of every day. Working? Focus on Jesus. Playing? Focus on Jesus. Do what you do every moment for Christ. Keep Him nearby, and your desire to enter into the realm of darkness will be lessened.

As I said, God's mercy toward us who sin and His compassion to those of us who are challenged by many trials, tribulations, and temptations is never ending. Understand, though, that we must, at some point, learn to live without sin dominating our lives. That is how we are able to rest under the yoke of Jesus Christ. It is the absence of guilt coupled with the reward of no punishment for that which we have done that allows us rest. Thank you, Jesus, for your sacrifice! But having these two things never relieves us of the responsibility to go and sin no more. Then we may truly relax for that *is* His burden—to take away the need for each of us to sin. When we were slaves to the law, our flesh cried out for sin for it was enslaved to sin for its satisfaction. Now Christ has come to us to free us from that need for we are able to find respite and peace within the confines of His wonderful presence. When we are found in Him, we cannot sin.

Jenny's incredible faithfulness to me is truly amazing to me simply because it is so rare. I have heard from many who work with dogs professionally that they don't have memory of past events, but they deal only in the *now*. I don't really think that's true simply because some animals remember people and behaviors, especially those that were threatening, but perhaps they remember even those that were kind and took great care for them. People do, and I am one who totally understands trauma and traumatic events in a professional as well as a personal level. Some things leave scars—both physical and mental—in both humans and animals. And that is exactly why I am amazed at Jenny's faithfulness. Her background should have scarred her irreparably. But her faith, her joy, and her constant look toward the future with hope has shown me that is exactly what the Lord desires of us.

Jenny believes that I will provide for her, love her, and protect her; and she, in return, waits for me. Whenever I need her, she is there and merely waits for instructions. If I were that way with God, every moment and every day, I would have such a wonderful peace that would never leave, even for a moment. I'm working on that. I think that part of the problem is that many of us are always on, always ready to go, and we never actually just sit and rest in the peace that passes understanding. It is an option, you know. Just take a break, bask in the joy of being in the presence of the King, and enjoy all He has given you.

CHAPTER EIGHTEEN

Always Amazed, but
Never Surprised

IN THE LAST chapter, I alluded to the fact that some of Jenny's behaviors were amazing to me. But please understand that although amazing, they are not surprising. You have by now, I am sure, picked up on the fact that Jenny owns an incredible joy that is unlike any animal I have known. Many people remark on her antics, whether it be rolling on her back for a belly rub or the way she prances everywhere she goes. And she has that permanent smile that washes over her face as she does almost anything involving humans.

It is this unending joy that gives her the ability to not only be amazing in her actions but amazed at life. The wonder of everything is built into her like no other being I have encountered. And that *is* a surprise to me. We should all be like that. God has certainly built the capacity to wonder and to search into every heart. But we often misplace that capacity and lay it aside in order to pursue other things. In other words, life gets in the way of our amazement. That is indeed sad for the only thing worth our total pursuit is but one thing. It is the pursuit of God.

Jenny has no way to conceive the presence of God for that has not been inserted into her being. But it is not a bad thing, for I think she has been a gift from God for me. Her constant concern for me is such a wonder, such an amazing wonder. As I consider her place in the totality of both our lives, I can see what a wonderful gift she is for she teaches me almost daily about life. Life is one constant adventure and then a nap. We seek the newest thing and then rest. Sometimes we rest along the way, and sometimes we just push on because there is so much to see. She cannot conceive that God has made both the honeybee and the flowers that the bee visits, floating, it seems, as it moves among them for some strange reason she is unable to discern. Still, she watches in amazement at the tiny creature who floats in the air. We should do the same.

If only we would look around us at the world in which we live and be amazed. The creatures the trees, the mountains, the hills, the valleys, the oceans, the rivers, the lakes, the planets, the stars, and the moon are all testament to the wonders of God. Stand and be amazed, but never be surprised for surprise could kill you—forever. The glory of God is all around, and only a fool misses it. Psalms 104 expresses it so beautifully, and the psalmist shows us why we should all be amazed at all the creation. I will include part of it here, but take the time to read the entire psalm and think about the moment of creation as the words come to your mind.

Psalms 104:2–12

> ²*You are dressed in a robe of light. You stretch out the starry curtain of the heavens;* ³*you lay out the rafters of your home in the rain clouds. You make the clouds your chariot; you ride upon the wings of the wind.* ⁴*The winds are your messengers; flames of fire are your servants.* ⁵*You placed the world on its foundation so it would never be moved.* ⁶*You clothed the earth with floods of water, water that covered even the mountains.* ⁷*At your command, the water fled; at the sound of your thunder, it hurried away.* ⁸*Mountains rose and valleys sank to the levels you decreed.* ⁹*Then you set a firm boundary for the seas, so they would never again cover the earth.* ¹⁰*You make springs pour water into the ravines, so streams gush down from the mountains.* ¹¹*They provide water for all the animals, and the wild donkeys quench their thirst.* ¹²*The birds nest beside the streams and sing among the branches of the trees.*

There are thirty-five verses in this psalm. And it shows how God has made everything work together to provide sustenance and enjoyment for the final, greatest creation God ever made, us. There was a plan. That is truly amazing. Every being, every tree, and every star are all put in place by the hand of God. And His desire is to share it all with us, forever.

That certainly amazes me. But it does not surprise me at all.

God is love. His Word declares that again and again and in so many ways that I won't even mention them. But trust me, it does. It's a whole other book. The fact that He does so many things for us should never surprise us for that is how love acts. It is what love does. I haven't been good at love in my life—at least the kind of love that God has shown us, and in particular, me. I have really excelled at loving myself, and that is to my shame. God has given each of us the ability to reach out beyond ourselves to love others at least as much as we love ourselves. There have been some who have lived who have shown that kind of love—people like William Booth and Mother Teresa—and the world looks on in amazement for that kind of love is rare. Were it not, the world would have no reason to be amazed. But much of the world is also surprised at such love for it does not exist where they are. And seeing it for the first time may yield an expression of disbelief.

Jenny has shown me through her particular brand of faithful love that it is something that exists in every creature at some level, and the level of love that she owns is on a level of godly love. I know I might offend some at this, but godly love is a love that is unfailing and unlimited. And that's the kind of love she shows. And when it comes down to it, it exists in many creatures God has created. And many creatures exhibit this type of love with much enthusiasm, but there is one of God's creatures that, although it has been created to be the most intelligent of all physical creations and, as a result, rules the earth, is the one most likely to refrain from showing the same love God has shown them to any other fellow creature. You figured it out, didn't you? It's us.

Among all creation, no other creature has such a penchant for evil. Humans can be filled with hatred and are able to manifest such absolute darkness in a moment's notice. I have seen this myself as someone turns from a reasonable, a seemingly kind, and a quiet person into a violent and raging monster in mere moments. And that's why God had to make a way to change that without destroying everyone. That way is twofold.

First, we must experience God's love. It always comes the same way the first time. It comes as mercy and forgiveness for everything we have ever done. We just have to come through the only door through which we are able to come to approach the living God: Jesus Christ. When that happens, a transformation begins, and the transforming part will take the rest of your life, for it is the Holy Spirit, the third person of the Godhead, who performs that transformational work. But make no mistake; we have a part in it.

We not only choose if we desire to partake but we also choose the depth of relationship we desire to chase. God is fullness in every aspect of life, both this mortal and temporary life as well as eternal life. Life is what He does. Once we begin the trek on the path toward God, He becomes addicting. He becomes fulfilling. He becomes everything. And when you realize that this one being is able to make everything in your life better, every relationship, every job you perform, every person you meet, the foods you eat, and even your suffering will be better. Don't you want your suffering to be better? It may not end, but it can be better endured.

Jenny showed me that when you really desire to be with someone, you will do whatever it takes to be with that person. You will wait in uncomfortable places, in the rain, and even in the snow as long as you are near your beloved. You will do things you don't want to do simply because the one you love has asked you to do them. You will sit and stare and meditate upon the one you love for the simple reason that you love them. You will be ashamed and walk the walk of shame when you let down your love for you are weak and cat food is a strong draw. And although your sin is great, you know that you will find mercy at the feet of your beloved (if you offer your belly to be rubbed).

We all have much to learn about relationships—our relationships with one another, our relationships with animals, and especially our relationship with God. And it seems like it is God that gets neglected more than any other. But I take heart in the fact that God has built into the heart of every creature a measure of love, and those creatures know instinctively that love held too tightly can never grow. It is only when we allow our love outside the boundaries of our own fists and toss it into not only our lives but the lives of others that we are able to experience the fullness of that love. Jenny has shown me that kind of love, and I am amazed. But I am certainly not surprised for the love she has shown me comes straight from the heart of God and has been poured out in her life.

If all of us would just take the time to look around at all the wonderful things God has placed nearby—the things we fail to notice on a regular basis and the things that actually make life worth living—and learn to cherish them, we may find that we have missed a lot. But it's never too late. We are all able to investigate the love that God has shown us as a whole and experience God's love for us individually. Just take some time and experience that love from all those who surround you—the furry ones and not so furry. Jenny has taught me that to love completely is the only way to love, and that is funny because Jesus said the same thing.

You may contact the author at
PO Box 1804, Show Low, AZ 85902
or through our website.

I hope this book has given you a few giggles as well as some food for thought so that your relationship with God will never cease from growing.

Be sure to check out our website at www.agalliao.net and take a look at our first book *Learning to Agalliao,* available everywhere as well as on the secure website Agalliao.net.

Made in the USA
Columbia, SC
19 October 2023

24695191R00074